Cambridge Elements ≡

Elements in the Philosophy of Religion
edited by
Yujin Nagasawa
University of Birmingham

THE ATONEMENT

William Lane Craig

Talbot School of Theology, Biola University
Houston Baptist University

CAMBRIDGE
UNIVERSITY PRESS

CAMBRIDGE
UNIVERSITY PRESS

University Printing House, Cambridge CB2 8BS, United Kingdom

One Liberty Plaza, 20th Floor, New York, NY 10006, USA

477 Williamstown Road, Port Melbourne, VIC 3207, Australia

314–321, 3rd Floor, Plot 3, Splendor Forum, Jasola District Centre, New Delhi – 110025, India

79 Anson Road, #06–04/06, Singapore 079906

Cambridge University Press is part of the University of Cambridge.

It furthers the University's mission by disseminating knowledge in the pursuit of education, learning, and research at the highest international levels of excellence.

www.cambridge.org
Information on this title: www.cambridge.org/9781108457408
DOI: 10.1017/9781108558020

First published 2018

A catalog record for this publication is available from the British Library.

ISBN 978-1-108-45740-8 Paperback
ISSN 2399-5165 (online)
ISSN 2515-9763 (print)

The Atonement

Elements in the Philosophy of Religion

DOI: 10.1017/9781108558020
First published online: June 2018

William Lane Craig
Talbot School of Theology, Biola University
Houston Baptist University

Abstract: *The Atonement* offers in a concise compass an inter-disciplinary approach to the complex doctrine of the atonement, drawing upon biblical studies, church history, and analytic philosophy. Divided into three parts, the book first treats the biblical basis of the doctrine of the atonement, an aspect of the doctrine not often taken with sufficient seriousness by contemporary Christian philosophers writing on the subject. The second part highlights some of the principal alternative theories of the atonement offered in the pre-modern era, with a view to accurately expositing these often misunderstood theories. Finally part three, drawing upon insights from the philosophy of law, defends a multi-faceted atonement theory which features penal substitution as a central element. By employing distinctions found in legal thought often overlooked in philosophical treatments of atonement, the author seeks to offer a philosophically coherent account of Christ's atonement that connects closely with the biblical doctrine of forensic justification.

Keywords: atonement, Christ, expiation, propitiation, penal substitution, substitutionary atonement, imputation, vicarious liability, justification, sacrifice, ransom, satisfaction

ISBNs: 9781108457408 (PB), 9781108558020 (OC)
ISSNs: 2399-5165 (online), 2515-9763 (print)

Contents

Bearing shame and scoffing rude,
In my place condemned He stood,
Sealed my pardon with His blood,
Hallelujah! What a Savior!

Guilty, vile, and helpless we;
Spotless Lamb of God was He;
"Full atonement!" Can it be?
Hallelujah! What a Savior!

Philip Bliss

Preface

Having pursued for several decades a long-term research program on the coherence of theism, I decided to interrupt my project by tackling the Christian doctrine of the atonement. I was aware that the Protestant Reformers' doctrine of Christ's substitutionary atonement faced formidable philosophical objections that few contemporary theologians seemed equipped (or willing!) to answer. I had hoped that Christian philosophers might take up the challenge, as they have done with other Christian doctrines such as the Trinity and incarnation. But I found myself disappointed and dissatisfied with the unbiblical and anemic theories of the atonement defended by many contemporary Christian philosophers. I wished that someone would step forward with a philosophically competent defense of the Protestant Reformers' doctrine of substitutionary atonement. The 500th anniversary of the Protestant Reformation made such a defense especially timely. Finally, I decided to tackle the subject myself.

The result has been unexpectedly rich. I thought I understood the doctrine of the atonement; indeed, I have taught on the subject. But I had no idea of the depths of fresh insight that this study would bring. As I delved into the doctrine of Christ's atonement – biblically, historically, philosophically – new understanding has been the reward.

Perhaps the most important insight biblically has been the gradual realization on my part that the term "atonement" is not univocal in its meaning. This fact, known to biblical theologians but not, generally, to Christian philosophers, subverts many philosophers' work on the atonement. For their theories are typically about atonement in the broad sense of *reconciliation*, whereas the biblical meaning of the Hebrew and Greek words translated by "atonement" and its cognates is *purgation* or *cleansing*. It turns out that many Christian philosophers' theories of the atonement are not theories of the atonement at all in the biblical sense.

Historically, I have been more than mildly surprised at how traditional atonement theories have been misrepresented in the secondary literature. I am not talking about those cheap caricatures of traditional theories as implying cosmic child abuse or hateful divine vengeance, but about responsible secondary literature. I first became aware of this distortion with regard to Anselm, who was accused of representing God as a feudal Lord too vain to overlook an insult. But then I realized that Abelard had also been misrepresented, and then Hugo Grotius, as well! One has only to read the primary sources themselves to realize how distorted an account of these thinkers' theories is often given in the secondary literature. Probably most surprising for me was the discovery that the Church Fathers were not uniformly committed to the ransom theory of the atonement but articulated views involving a wide variety of motifs.

But it is philosophically that this study has proved most rewarding. I had never delved into the philosophy of law prior to commencing this study. But I soon realized that it is in the philosophy of law that theories of punishment are most discussed, as well as theories of justice. Any adequate discussion of the doctrine of penal substitution and the challenges to it must take account of the legal literature on justice, punishment, and pardon. Not that theology should mirror our system of justice – far from it! – but rather that, given the forensic or judicial motifs that characterize the New Testament, interesting and fruitful analogies and parallels to theological doctrines may be found in our justice system. These may provide support for the coherence or justice of various Christian doctrines. Those who claim, for example, that we know nothing of the imputation of someone's responsibility or guilt for wrongdoing to another innocent party are just ignorant of the law. Again and again, I have been amazed at the theological insight that emerges from a study of legal philosophy and the law.

In order to make this Element accessible to biblical scholars, theologians, and philosophers alike, I have tried to presuppose as little as is feasible about each discipline. This necessitates explaining, e.g., what the Septuagint is for the sake of Christian philosophers and what retributive justice is for the sake of biblical theologians. My hope is that specialists familiar with one discipline may still find much to learn in another.

With regard to the law, I am especially grateful to Dr. Descheemaeker of the University of Edinburgh School of Law for helping to direct me to legal literature on various subjects and to Shaun McNaughton at Brown & Streza LLP for help in obtaining court opinions. I'm also grateful to my research assistant Timothy Bayless for procuring for me research materials, as well as proofreading. As always, I am thankful for my wife Jan's faithful support and interest in this subject.

Finally, I thank Professor Yujin Nagasawa for his inviting me to contribute this volume to the Cambridge Elements of Philosophy series. Due to the severe word limit, this Element is necessarily very succinct, though, I think, accurate. I hope to publish a fuller, more detailed discussion in the near future.

William Lane Craig
Atlanta, Georgia

Introduction

The word "atonement" is unique among theological terms, being a derivation, not from Greek or Latin, but from Middle English, namely, the phrase "at onement," designating a state of harmony. The closest New Testament (NT) word for atonement in this sense is *katallagē* or reconciliation, specifically reconciliation between God and man.[1] Reconciliation is the overarching theme of the NT, and other important NT motifs such as the Kingdom of God, salvation, justification, and redemption are subservient to it. Atonement in this sense thus lies at the heart of the Christian faith.

But there is a narrower sense of "atonement" that is expressed by the biblical words typically translated by this English word. In the Old Testament (OT), "atonement" and its cognates translate words having the Hebrew root "*kpr*." Best known of these expressions is doubtless *Yom Kippur*, the Day of Atonement. To atone in this sense takes as its object sin or impurity and has the sense "to purify, to cleanse." The Greek equivalent in the Septuagint (LXX) and NT is *hilaskesthai*. While the result of atonement in this narrow sense may be said to be atonement in the broad sense, nevertheless the biblical words translated as "atonement" or "to atone" need to be understood in the narrower sense if we are to understand the meaning of the texts. Theologically, the doctrine of the atonement concerns atonement primarily in the narrower, biblical sense of cleansing of sin and has traditionally been treated under the priestly work of Christ.[2]

The message of the NT is that God, out of His great love, has provided the means of atonement for sin through Christ's death: "For God so loved the world that he gave his only Son, that whoever believes in him should not perish but have eternal life" (Jn 3.16). By his death on the cross, Christ has made possible the reconciliation of alienated and condemned sinners to God. Thus, "the cross"

---

[1] See II Cor 5.17–20; also Rom 5.10–11; Col 1.19–23; Eph 2. On the centrality of the theme of reconciliation to the NT message, see Marshall (2007, ch. 4).

[2] In contrast, Eleonore Stump (2018) treats atonement in a very broad sense, as signaled by her use of "*at onement*," designating a state of union with God. Accordingly, her book is not about Christology, but about soteriology and, especially, pneumatology. The Holy Spirit displaces Christ as the central figure in her account of achieving union with God. The death of Christ plays a relatively minor role in her theory of *at onement*, and atonement in the narrow sense no role at all.

came to be a metaphor epitomizing the Gospel message, such that Paul could call the Gospel "the word of the cross" (I Cor 1.18).

So the four Gospels devote disproportionate space to Jesus's so-called passion, the final week of his suffering and crucifixion, thereby emphasizing his death. Of course, Jesus's death is not the end of the passion story: the Gospels all conclude with the proclamation of Jesus's victorious resurrection, vindicating him as God's chosen one. The death and resurrection of Jesus are two sides of the same coin: he "was put to death for our trespasses and raised for our justification" (Rom 4.25).

Paul quotes the earliest summary of the Gospel message, a four-line formula dating to within five years of Jesus's crucifixion, reminding the Corinthian believers:

> I delivered to you as of first importance what I also received:
>
> > that Christ died for our sins in accordance with the Scriptures,
> > and that he was buried,
> > and that he was raised on the third day in accordance with the
> > Scriptures,
> > and that he appeared to Cephas, then to the Twelve.
>
> (I Cor 15.3–5)

This is the message, Paul says, that was proclaimed by all the apostles (I Cor 15.11), and it is the message that dominates the NT.

Notice that Christ is said to have died "for our sins" and to have been put to death (or delivered up) "for our trespasses." How is it that Jesus's death dealt with our sins? How did his death on the cross overcome the estrangement and condemnation of sinners before a holy God, so as to reconcile them to him?

In handling this question, we should distinguish between the *fact* of the atonement and a *theory* of the atonement. A great variety of theories of the atonement have been offered to make sense of the fact that Christ, by his death, has provided the means of reconciliation with God. Competing theories of the atonement need to be assessed by (i) their accord with biblical teaching and (ii) their philosophical coherence. Unfortunately, the work of contemporary Christian philosophers on the doctrine of the atonement has been largely uninformed by biblical exegesis. Theories of the atonement are laid out based on the way in which reconciliation is typically achieved in human relationships. If the biblical texts are discussed at all, it is only after a theory of the atonement has been laid out, which is then read back into the biblical texts.

Not only does such a methodology risk distortion because of the enormous disanalogies between merely human relationships and divine–human relationships, but more fundamentally it runs the risk of developing a theory of the atonement that, however congenial, just is not a Christian theory of the atonement because it does not accord with the biblical data. Such an approach to the biblical texts represents eisegesis, not exegesis. So flawed a hermeneutic will not deliver to us the meaning of the author of the text but only our own preconceived views. Because the biblical data concerning the atonement are so often neglected by Christian philosophers, we need to begin with a survey of some of the key biblical atonement motifs.

1 Biblical Data concerning the Atonement

Theologians have often remarked on the multiplicity of metaphors and motifs characterizing the atonement found in the NT. Here we want to survey some of the essential elements that make up the biblical doctrine of the atonement. If any of these go missing from a theory of the atonement, then we know that we do not have a biblical theory of the atonement. We may then be spared the digression of pursuing such a theory further, since it is disqualified as a Christian atonement theory.

Our interest in examining the biblical material is not in historical-critical analysis of the biblical text, seeking, for example, to determine the date and provenance of the priestly traditions concerning the Jewish sacrifices or to ascertain the authentic words of Jesus concerning his death, but rather with the biblical text as we have it.

In approaching the biblical teaching on the atonement, we must decide whether to approach the subject thematically or by author. While the latter approach has the advantage of giving us a clearer picture of what a Paul or a John, for example, thought about the subject, it does not permit us to develop common emphases. We shall therefore take a thematic approach to the biblical materials.

1.1 Sacrifice

The predominant motif used in the NT to characterize the atonement is the presentation of Christ's death as a sacrificial offering to God on our behalf. NT scholar Joel Green provides a pithy summary:

> In their development of the saving significance of Jesus' death, early Christians were heavily influenced by the world of the sacrificial cult in Israel's Scriptures and by the practices of animal sacrifice in the Jerusalem temple – The expression "*Christ died for all*," widespread in this and variant forms throughout the NT (e.g., Mk 14:24; Rom 5:6, 8; 15:3; Gal 2:21; 1 Pet 3:18), is thematic in this regard, as are references to the salvific effects of *the blood of Christ* (e.g., Acts 20:28; Rom 5:9; Col 1:20). Jesus' death is

presented as a *covenant sacrifice* (e.g., Mk 14:24; 1 Cor 11:25; Heb 7:22; 8:6; 9:15), a *Passover sacrifice* (e.g., Jn 19:14; 1 Cor 5:7–8), the *sin offering* (Rom 8:3; 2 Cor 5:21), the *offering of first fruits* (1 Cor 15:20, 23), the sacrifice offered on *the Day of Atonement* (Heb 9–10), and an offering reminiscent of *Abraham's presentation of Isaac* (e.g., Rom 8:32). The writer of Ephesians summarizes well: "Christ loved us and gave himself up for us, a fragrant offering and sacrifice to God." (Eph 5:2)[3]

1.1.1 Jesus's Attitude toward His Death

The interpretation of Jesus's death as a sacrificial offering was not an ex post facto rationalization on the part of Christians of Jesus's ignominious fate. Rather, Jesus himself had seen his impending death in this light. He predicted his death (Mk 10.33–34) and even provoked it by his Messianic actions in Jerusalem (Mk 11.1–10, 15–18). Jesus's selection of the Passover festival as the time of the climax of his ministry was no accident. For as he celebrated with his disciples his final Passover meal, "he took bread . . . and gave it to them, and said, 'Take; this is my body.' And he took a cup and . . . gave it to them, and they all drank of it. And he said to them, 'This is my blood of the covenant, which is poured out for many'" (Mk 14.22–24). Jesus saw his death symbolized in the elements of the Passover meal. It was the blood of the Passover lamb, smeared on the doorposts of Jewish homes, that had saved the Jewish people from God's judgment in Egypt. Moreover, the expression "this is my blood of the covenant" recalls Moses's words at the inauguration of the old covenant (Exod 24.8). Jesus the Messiah is inaugurating, by his death, the new covenant prophesied by Jeremiah (Jer 31.31–34), which would bring restoration and forgiveness of sin. Moreover, the words "poured out for many" hark back to Isaiah's prophecy of the Servant of the LORD, who

> poured out his soul to death,
>   and was numbered with the transgressors;
> yet he bore the sin of many,
>   and made intercession for the transgressors.
>   (Is 53.12)

Jesus saw himself as the suffering Servant of Isaiah 53, who "makes himself an offering for sin" (Is 53.10). Earlier, Jesus had said of himself, "the Son of man also came not to be served but to serve, and to give his life as a ransom for many" (Mk 10.45). The Son of Man is a divine–human figure from Daniel's prophecy whom "all peoples, nations, and languages should serve" (Dan 7.14). In his

---

[3] Green (2006, p. 172, my emphases).

paradoxical statement, Jesus stands things on their head, declaring that the Son of Man has come in the role of a servant and, like the Servant of Isaiah 53, gives his life as a ransom for many. Jesus evidently saw his death as a redemptive sacrifice, like the Passover sacrifice, and himself as a sin bearer, inaugurating, like the Mosaic sacrifice, a fresh covenant between God and the people.

1.1.2 OT Background

We can gain insight into Jesus's death as a sacrificial offering by examining the function of the OT sacrifices that formed the interpretive framework for Jesus's death. In doing so, we enter a world that is utterly foreign to modern Western readers. Most of us have never seen an animal slaughtered, much less done it ourselves, and, accustomed as we are to buying our meat and poultry in anti-septically wrapped packaging in refrigerated bins, we are apt to find the animal sacrifices described in the OT revolting. Moreover, most of us have no familiarity with a world in which ritual practices fraught with symbolic meaning play a major role in one's interactions with the spiritual realm, and so the OT cult may strike us as bizarre and opaque. If we are to understand these practices, we need to shed our Western sensibilities and try to enter sympathetically into the world of a bucolic society that was not squeamish about blood and guts, and which had a highly developed ritual system in its approach to God.

The challenge of understanding these ancient texts is compounded by the fact that they often describe rituals without explaining their meaning, which was probably well known to their contemporary practitioners. Therefore, we must try as best we can to discern their proper interpretation based upon the clues that we have. Fortunately, we have sufficient evidence to form some reliable ideas about what the sacrifices were intended to accomplish.

The OT sacrifices come in a bewildering variety, the distinctive functions of which are not always clear.[4] Fortunately, we can determine the general function of the sacrifices without going into a delineation of the various kinds that were prescribed. In general, the sacrifices filled the twin fundamental purposes of expiation of sin or impurity and propitiation of God. "To expiate" means *to remove, to annul, to cancel*; "to propitiate" means *to appease, to placate, to satisfy*. The object of expiation is sin/impurity; the object of propitiation is God.

---

[4] A popular account may be found in Morris (1983, ch. 2). For detailed, scholarly discussion, see Milgrom (1991, pp. 133–72). We have little knowledge of sacrifices outside the Levitical system. The so-called burnt offering seems to have existed prior to its incorporation into the Levitical sacrificial system and was offered both to propitiate God (Gen 8.21) and to expiate sin (Job 1.5; 42.8)

1.1.2.1   Propitiatory Sacrifices

At least some of the OT sacrifices were clearly propitiatory. A premier example is the sacrifice of the Passover lamb. This sacrifice was not originally instituted for the purpose of expiation; rather, the blood of the lamb smeared on the doorframes of Israelite homes served to shelter them as God's judgment swept over Egypt (Exod 12.13). Had they not offered the sacrifices, God's deadly judgment would have fallen on the Israelites, as well.

Propitiation is also in view in the various priestly sacrifices offered in the Tabernacle (and later, in the Temple). The careful regulations concerning the sacrificial offerings are to be understood against the background of God's striking down Aaron's sons for their unlawful offering of sacrifices in the Tabernacle precincts (Lev 10.1–2; 16.1). God was conceived to be specially present in the innermost sanctum of the Tabernacle, which therefore had to be approached with utmost care. It was a dangerous business to have a holy God dwelling in the midst of a sinful and impure people, as we see in God's warning to the people of Israel: "You are a stiff-necked people; if for a single moment I should go up among you, I would consume you" (Exod 33.5). The sacrificial system functioned to facilitate the juxtaposition of the holy and the unholy. It did this, not merely by purging the Tabernacle and its paraphernalia of impurity, but also by propitiating God and so averting His wrath upon the people. The roasting of the sacrificial animals, in particular, is repeatedly said to produce "a pleasing odor to the LORD" (e.g., Lev 1.9), which implies that the sacrifices helped to cultivate God's favor (cf. Gen 8.21).

1.1.2.2   Expiatory Sacrifices

Certain OT sacrifices also served an expiatory function. In the priestly system of sacrifices, the sacrificial offerings served to remove ceremonial impurity and/or moral guilt.[5] Some commentators have overemphasized the function of the sacrifices in purifying the Tabernacle and its sacred objects to the neglect of the sacrifices' role in cleansing the people themselves of guilt and impurity. Reducing the function of the sacrifices to the cleansing of objects alone is implausible and fails to do justice to the biblical text. For purging objects of impurity while leaving the worshippers themselves guilty and unclean would fail to address the root of the problem. Moreover, the text repeatedly promises,

---

[5] Three broad categories of sin were recognized: unintentional sins, intentional sins short of apostasy, and intentional sins of apostasy. The Levitical personal sacrifices availed for expiation of sins only of the first two types; persons committing "high-handed" sins were to be cut off from the people, unless through the intercession of a mediator (such as Moses) God should pardon them (Sklar 2015). The fact that sins could be thus pardoned without sacrifice suggests already that the animal sacrifices served a ritual or symbolic function (Heb 10.1–4).

"the priest shall make atonement on your behalf for the sin that you have committed, and you shall be forgiven" (Lev 4.35; cf. 4.20, 26, 31, *etc.*). The word translated "make atonement" (*kippēr*) has a range of meanings – to purge, to ransom, to expiate – but what is significant here is the result: *the person's sins are forgiven*. The ritual sacrifice has removed his guilt.

In his acclaimed *Leviticus* commentary, Jacob Milgrom advises, "Although the cult concentrates heavily on the purging of sanctuary impurity, it too recognizes that the ultimate source of impurity is human sin" (Milgrom 1991, pp. 1083–84). Sin must therefore be expiated. The continual purging and re-consecration of the altar "points to the singular function of the altar: it is the medium of God's salvific expiation of the sins of Israel. Therefore, not only does it have to be purged of Israel's sins; it must be a fit instrument for effecting expiation for Israel when sacrifices are offered up on it" (1991, p. 1038). While repentance is a necessary condition of God's forgiveness of a sin, "For the complete annulment of the sin, however, for the assurance of divine forgiveness (*sālaḥ*), sacrificial expiation (*kippēr*) is a*lways* required" (1991, p. 377). *Kippēr* in its most abstract sense thus comes to mean *atone* or *expiate*. "The meaning here is that the offerer is cleansed of his impurities/sins and becomes reconciled, 'at one,' with God" (1991, p. 1083).

The personal Levitical animal offerings were accompanied by a telling hand-laying ritual. The offerer of the animal sacrifice was to lay his hand upon the animal's head before slaying it (Lev 1.4). The Hebrew expression *sāmak yādô* indicates a forceful laying of the hand: one was to press his hand upon the head of the beast to be sacrificed. Although Milgrom has suggested that this "hand-leaning" ritual was meant merely to indicate ownership of the sacrificial animal (Milgrom 1991, pp. 151–52), such an interpretation is implausible and trivializes an apparently important feature of the ceremony. Someone pulling an animal by a rope around its neck before the altar is just as obviously the person bringing his sacrifice as someone who carries in his hand a bird or grain for sacrifice, and if there were any doubt a verbal affirmation would suffice. Rather, this emphatic gesture is plausibly meant to indicate the identification of the offerer with the animal, so that the animal's fate symbo-lizes his own. Death is the penalty for sin, and the animal dies in place of the worshipper. This is not to say that the animal was punished in the place of the worshipper; rather the animal suffered the fate that would have been the worshipper's punishment had it happened to him. The priest's sprinkling the blood of the sacrifice on the altar, whatever its exact meaning, indicates minimally that the animal's life has been offered to God as a sacrifice to atone for the offerer's sin.

1.1.2.3   Yom Kippur Sacrifices

The expiatory ritual par excellence was the annual sacrifices on Yom Kippur (Day of Atonement), which was performed on behalf of the whole nation and covered a wider range of sins than did the personal sacrifices (Lev 16). This day featured an extraordinary ritual involving the presentation of a pair of goats, one of which was sacrificially killed and the other driven out into the desert, bearing away the iniquities of the people, which had been symbolically laid on the goat through a hand-laying ritual performed by the priest. These actions are best seen as two aspects of the same ritual rather than as separate rituals (Ruane 2016). In a similar ritual involving two birds offered for the cleansing of impurity (Lev 14.2–7), the blood of the slain bird cleanses the person while the release of the other bird symbolizes the removal of his impurity. The case of the two goats is analogous. If sin could be expiated simply by laying it on a goat and driving it away into the desert, then the whole sacrificial system would become pointless. Rather, a sacrificial death is necessary: "For the life of the flesh is in the blood; and I have given it for you upon the altar to make atonement for your souls; for it is the blood that makes atonement, by reason of the life" (Lev 17.11).

The description of the Yom Kippur ritual differentiates between "mak[ing] atonement for the sanctuary, and . . . for the tent of meeting and for the altar" and "mak[ing] atonement for the priests and for all the people" (Lev 16.33). Making atonement for inanimate objects is to purge them of ritual uncleanness; making atonement for persons is to expiate their sins. "For on this day shall atonement be made for you, to cleanse you; from all your sins you shall be clean before the LORD" (v 30). The sprinkled blood of the goat, along with the blood of a bull sacrificed by the priest, shall not only "make atonement for the sanctuary" but also "make atonement for himself and for his house and for all the assembly of Israel" (vv 16–17). Once the altar has also been suitably purged, the priest may then "offer his burnt offering and the burnt offering of the people, and make atonement for himself and for the people" (v 24). Thus, the blood of the sacrificial goat atones for the sins of the people while the driving out of the other symbolizes the efficacy of the sacrifice in expiating their sin.

1.1.3 Christ as Sacrifice

When we return to the NT construal of Jesus's death as a sacrificial offering, it is worth bearing in mind that what ultimately matters for the doctrine of the atonement is not how the sacrifices may have been originally understood but how the NT authors understood them. For example, the author of Hebrews says flatly, "It is impossible that the blood of bulls and goats should take away sins" (Heb 10.4). He thereby reveals his understanding of the OT sacrifices as intended, at least, to expiate sin and his view of Christ's self-sacrifice as truly expiatory. The NT authors did not think of Christ on the analogy of a bloodless scapegoat or grain offering but focused on the animal sacrifices, the author of Hebrews going so far as to say that "without the shedding of blood there is no forgiveness of sins" (Heb 9.22).

The NT writers think of Christ's death as both expiatory and propitiatory. With regard to the expiation of sin, the author of Hebrews hammers home the point that in contrast to the OT sacrifices, "which can never take away sins" (10.11), Christ, "having been offered once to bear the sins of many" (9.28), "remove[d] sin by the sacrifice of himself" (9.26), so that "we have been sanctified through the offering of the body of Jesus Christ once for all" (10.10). John presents Christ as a Passover lamb whose death, in contrast to the original Passover sacrifice, is expiatory: "Behold, the Lamb of God, who takes away the sin of the world!" (Jn 1.29). Paul uses technical Levitical terminology to refer to Christ as "a sin offering" (*peri hamartias*) (Rom 8.3; cf. Heb. 10.6, 8). Those who have believed in Christ "have been justified by his blood" (Rom 5.9). Christ's righteous act of obedience "leads to acquittal and life for all men. For ... by one man's obedience many will be made righteous" (5.18–19).

With regard to propitiation, the protracted debate over the linguistic meaning of *hilastērion* in Rom 3.25, "whom God put forward as a *hilastērion* in his blood,"[6] has unfortunately diverted attention from the conceptual necessity of propitiation in Paul's thinking. Whatever word Paul might have used here – had he written, for example, *peri hamartias*, as in Rom 8.3, instead of *hilastērion* – the context would still require that Christ's death provide the solution to the problem described in chapters 1–3. Paul's crowning statement concerning Christ's atoning death (Rom 3.21–26) comes against the backdrop of his exposition of God's wrath upon and condemnation of mankind for its

---

[6] For an overview of the debate, see Bailey (forthcoming). It is not disputed that we find quite different meanings of *hilastērion* in the LXX and in extra-biblical Greek literature, including the literature of Hellenistic Judaism. What is disputed is which is the relevant meaning of the word as used by Paul on this one occasion. The predominant meaning in extra-biblical literature is "propitiation" or "propitiatory offering." Especially noteworthy are the deaths of the Maccabean martyrs, which allayed God's wrath upon Israel (2 Macc 7.38), and thus served as "a propitiatory offering" (4 Macc 17.22 codex S; cf. *Sibylline Oracles* 3.625–28, where God is propitiated by the sacrifice of hundreds of bulls and lambs). This case belies any claims that *hilastēria* had to be concrete, inanimate objects. The LXX, on the other hand, uses *hilastērion* to refer to the *kapporet* or lid of the ark of the covenant, where the blood of the Yom Kippur sacrifice was splashed, or, more widely, to altar faces where sacrificial blood was smeared (Ezek 43.14, 17, 20; Amos 9.1). On this interpretation Christ is the locus of atonement for sin.

sin. Something in Paul's ensuing exposition of Christ's death must solve this problem, averting God's wrath and rescuing us from the death sentence hanging over us. The solution is found in Christ, "whom God put forward as a *hilastērion* in his blood" (3.25).

Even if we take *hilastērion* to carry here its LXX meaning as opposed to its extra-biblical meaning, Paul is obviously using the expression metaphorically – Christ is not literally a piece of Temple furniture! Taken metaphorically rather than literally, however, the expression could convey a rich variety of connotations associated with sacrifice and atonement, so that the sort of dichotomistic reading forced by literal meanings becomes inappropriate. Paul was a Hellenistic Jew, whose writings bear the imprint of Hellenistic Jewish thought (e.g., the natural theology of Rom 1 or the Logos doctrine behind Rom 11.36), and he might have expected his Roman readers to understand *hilastērion* in the customary sense. At the same time, by borrowing an image from the Day of Atonement rituals, Paul also conveys to his hearers the OT notion of expiation by blood sacrifice. Thomas Heicke comments that already in the OT, "by means of abstraction, the ritual itself turns into a metaphor," thus building "the basis and starting point for multiple transformations and further abstractions as well as metaphorical charging in Judaism . . . and Christianity (Rom 3:25: Christ as *hilasterion* – expiation or sacrifice of atonement, etc.)" (Heicke 2016).

Christ's death is thus both expiatory and propitiatory: "Since, therefore, we are now justified by his blood, much more shall we be saved by him from the wrath of God" (5.9). Given the manifold effects of Christ's blood, *hilastērion* is doubtlessly multivalent in Paul's usage, comprising both expiation and propitiation, so that a vague translation, for example, "an atoning sacrifice," is about the best one can give (cf. Heb 2.17; 1 Jn 2.2; 4.10).

1.2 Isaiah's Servant of the Lord

Another significant NT motif concerning Christ's death is Isaiah's Servant of the Lord. NT authors saw Jesus as the suffering Servant described in Is 52.13–53.12. Ten of the twelve verses of Isaiah 53 are quoted in the NT, which also abounds in allusions and echoes of this passage. I have already mentioned the Synoptic Gospels' accounts of Jesus's words at the Last Supper. In Acts 8.30–35, Philip, in response to an Ethiopian official's question concerning Isaiah 53 – "About whom does the prophet speak?" – shares "the good news about Jesus." I Peter 2.22–25 is a reflection on Christ as the Servant of Isaiah 53, who "bore our sins in his body on the tree." Hebrews 9.28 alludes to Is 53.12 in describing Christ as "having been offered once to bear the sins of many." The influence of Isaiah 53 is also evident in Romans, I and II Corinthians, Galatians, Philippians, I Timothy, and

Titus. NT scholar William Farmer concludes, "This evidence indicates that there is an Isaianic soteriology deeply embedded in the New Testament which finds its normative form and substance in Isaiah 53" (Farmer 1998, p. 267; cf. Bailey 1998 and Watts 1998).

What is remarkable, even startling, about the Servant of Isaiah 53 is that he suffers substitutionally for the sins of others. Some scholars have denied this, claiming that the Servant merely shares in the punitive suffering of the Jewish exiles. But such an interpretation does not make as good sense of the shock expressed at what Yahweh has done in afflicting His Servant (Is 52.14–53.1,10) and is less plausible in light of the strong contrasts, reinforced by the Hebrew pronouns, drawn between the Servant and the persons speaking in the first-person plural:

> Surely he has borne our griefs
>> and carried our sorrows;
> yet we esteemed him stricken,
>> smitten by God, and afflicted.
> But he was wounded for our transgressions,
>> he was bruised for our iniquities;
> upon him was the chastisement that made us whole,
>> and with his stripes we are healed.
> All we like sheep have gone astray;
>> we have turned every one to his own way;
> and the LORD has laid on him
>> the iniquity of us all.
>
> (Is 53.4–6)[7]

We may compare the LORD's symbolically laying the punishment of Israel and Judah upon the prophet Ezekiel, so that he could be said to "bear their punishment" (Ezek 4.4–6). Here, in Isaiah 53, the Servant's bearing the punishment for Israel's sins is, however, not symbolic but real.

The idea of substitutionary suffering is, as we have seen, already implicit in the animal sacrifices prescribed in Leviticus. Death is the consequence of sin, and the animal dies in the place of the sinner. By the hand-laying ritual that precedes the sacrifice, the worshipper symbolically indicates his identification with the animal that he will sacrifice. This identification should not be thought of in terms of a magical penetration of the worshipper's soul into the animal, but in substitutionary terms. The animal's death is symbolic of the sinner's death. Thus, the animal "shall be accepted for him to make atonement

---

[7] See Hermisson (2004) and Hofius (2004), who says that substitutionary punishment "is expressed several times in the passage and should undoubtedly be seen as its dominant and central theme" (Hofius 2004, p. 164).

for him" (Lev 1.4). Similarly, in Isaiah 53 the Servant is said "to make himself an offering for sin" (v 10).

It is sometimes said that the idea of offering a human substitute is utterly foreign to Judaism; but this is, in fact, not true. The idea of substitutionary punishment is clearly expressed in Moses's offer to the LORD to be killed in place of the people, who had apostatized, in order to "make atonement" for their sin (Exod 32.30–34). Although Yahweh rejects Moses's offer of a substitutionary atonement, saying that "when the day comes for punishment, I will punish them for their sin" (v 34), the offer is nonetheless clear, and Yahweh simply declines the offer but does not dismiss it as absurd or impossible. Similarly, while Yahweh consistently rejects human sacrifice, in contrast to the practice of pagan nations, the story of God's commanding Abraham to sacrifice his son Isaac (whom the NT treats as a type of Christ) shows that such a thing is not impossible (Gen 22.1–19). In Isaiah 53, moreover, the idea of the Servant's substitutionary suffering is treated as extraordinary and surprising. The LORD has inflicted on His righteous Servant what He refused to inflict on Isaac and Moses.

The suffering of the Servant is agreed on all hands to be punitive. In the OT, the expression "to bear sin," when used of people, typically means *to be held culpable* or *to endure punishment* (e.g., Lev 5.1; 7.18; 19.8; 24.15; Num 5.31; 9.13; 14.34). The Servant does not bear his own sins, but the sins of others (vv 4, 11–12). Intriguingly, the phrase can be used regarding the priests' action of making atonement (e.g., Lev 10.17: "that you may bear the iniquity of the congregation, to make atonement for them before the LORD"). But the priests, unlike the Servant, do not suffer in so doing. The punitive nature of the Servant's suffering is clearly expressed in phrases like "wounded for our transgressions," "bruised for our iniquities," "upon him was the chastisement that made us whole," "the LORD has laid on him the iniquity of us all," and "stricken for the transgression of my people" (vv 5, 6, 8). This fact also serves to distinguish the Servant's sin-bearing from that of the scapegoat, which was merely the symbolic vehicle for the removal of sin.

By bearing the punishment due the people, the Servant reconciles them to God. While *kpr* language is not used, the concept is clearly present. The Servant, by his suffering, brings wholeness and healing (v 5), he makes "many to be accounted righteous" (v 11), and he makes "intercession for the transgressors" (v 12).

Returning to the NT, we find Christian authors interpreting Jesus as the sin-bearing Servant of Isaiah 53: "He himself bore our sins in his body on the tree, that we might die to sin and live to righteousness. By his wounds you have been healed" (I Pet 2.24). In light of Isaiah 53, texts like "Christ died for our sins in accordance with the Scriptures" (I Cor 15.3), ambiguous when taken in isolation, become pregnant with meaning. There is no other passage in the Jewish scriptures that could be construed as even remotely about the Messiah's dying for people's sins. The formulaic expression "died for our sins" thus refers to substitutionary, punitive suffering.[8] II Cor 5.21, "For our sake he made him to be sin who knew no sin, so that in him we might become the righteousness of God," is seen to echo in all its parts Is 53. "Who knew no sin" recalls "the righteous one, my servant," in whose mouth was no deceit (vv 9, 11); "for our sake he made him to be sin" recalls "the LORD has laid on him the iniquity of us all" (v 6); "in him we might become the righteousness of God" recalls "the righteous one, my servant, [shall] make many to be accounted righteous" (v 11). Again, no other OT passage remotely approaches the content of this sentence.

The NT authors, then, following Jesus in his own self-understanding, saw Christ as the suffering Servant of Isaiah 53, who suffered in the place of sinners, bearing the punishment they deserved that they might be reconciled to God.

1.3 Divine Justice

A third important motif concerning the atonement, prominent in the letters of Paul, is divine justice. We are not interested in Paul's doctrine of justification by faith, since that does not concern the atonement itself but rather the appropriation of its benefits. We want to inquire about the role of divine justice in the act of atonement. Paul's exposition of the way in which Christ's death achieves reconciliation with God is suffused with forensic terminology rooted in Jewish notions of law and justice.

1.3.1 OT Justice Motifs

In the OT, God is addressed with the legal title "Judge" (Gen 18.25) and acts rightly in that capacity. Moreover, He is not only the Judge; He is also the lawgiver. The heart of OT Judaism was the divine Torah (law) that governed all of life and man's relationship to God. Leon Morris reckons that of the 220 uses of *tôrah* in the OT, only 17 are clearly not about God's law. Of the 127 occurrences of *hōq* (statute), 87 are linked with the LORD; *huqqah*, another word for statute, is similarly linked in 96 out of 104 cases. *Mishpāt*, which is linked with the LORD about 180 times, is the usual term for 'judgment' and in its

---

[8] This meaning of "for" (*hyper*) is made clear by expressions like "delivered up for our trespasses" (Rom 4.25), where "for" translates *dia* + the accusative, meaning "on account of," and "delivered up" and "trespasses" recalls Is 53. 7–8; similarly, Mk 10.45, where "for" translates *anti*, meaning "instead of," "in exchange of."

participial form is used to refer to God as Judge. It may also mean *law.* Even the notion of a covenant (*berith*) is the notion of a legal contract. It is intriguing how OT writers often prefer legal to any other imagery when they are referring to what God does (e.g., Mic 6.1–2; Is 3.13; 41.21). The use of legal categories with respect to God in the OT, says Morris, "is frequent, so frequent indeed that it is plain that it corresponds to something deep-seated in Hebrew thinking. Law and the LORD went together" (Morris 1983, p. 181). In fact, it would be difficult to find a religion more wedded to legal categories than OT Judaism.

1.3.2 NT Justice Motifs

So the NT is filled with judicial language reflective of its Jewish background. By Morris' count, the NT has 92 examples of the noun *dikaiosynē* ("justice" or "righteousness"); 39 of the verb *dikaioō* (to "justify" or "reckon righteous"); ten of the noun *dikaiōma* ("ordinance" or "sentence of justification"); 81 of the adjective *dikaios* ("just" or "righteous"); and five of the adverb *dikaiōs* ("justly" or "righteously"). Paul blends cultic and judicial terminology in characterizing Christ's death:

> But now, apart from law, the righteousness of God has been disclosed, and is attested by the law and the prophets, the righteousness of God through faith in Jesus Christ for all who believe. For there is no distinction, since all have sinned and fall short of the glory of God; they are now justified by his grace as a gift, through the redemption that is in Christ Jesus, whom God put forward as a sacrifice of atonement by his blood, effective through faith. He did this to show his righteousness, because in his divine forbearance he had passed over the sins previously committed; it was to prove at the present time that he himself is righteous and that he justifies the one who has faith in Jesus. (Rom 3.21–26)

The NRSV translation alternates between righteousness terminology and justice terminology. One could have used righteousness terminology throughout by adopting Paul's expression "reckon righteous" from Rom 4.3, 23–24 instead of "justify," so as to read: "they are now reckoned righteous by his grace." On the other hand, using justice terminology throughout would make clear Paul's wordplay in v 26: God is both "just and the justifier."

1.3.2.1 Righteousness of God

1.3.2.1.1 Attribute or Gift?

Classically, there has been a debate over whether the expression *dikaiōsynē theou* ("righteousness" or "justice of God") refers to an attribute of God Himself or to the righteousness He reckons to believers. It is clear, I think, that the expression is multivalent. "The righteousness of God through faith" clearly refers to reckoned righteousness, since God's attribute is not "through faith." But just as clearly, "he himself is righteous" designates a property God Himself has.

1.3.2.1.2 New Perspective on Paul

Recently, a new debate about this expression has risen as a result of the so-called "new perspective on Paul," which construes God's righteousness in terms of His covenant faithfulness. If one adopts a reductive analysis of God's righteousness as His covenant faithfulness, this will radically impact one's understanding of Paul's atonement doctrine, for then justification is about God's reckoning to us covenant faithfulness, which makes dubious sense and, in any case, would not avail for salvation (Philip 3.6–9). Such a reductionistic interpretation has, however, been shown to be lexicographically untenable (Irons 2015). The implausibility of such a reductionism is perhaps best seen by asking what the opposite of righteousness – that is, unrighteousness – is said to be. It is not unfaithfulness, but wickedness and ungodliness (Rom 1.18). Faithlessness is but one of the litany of sins listed by Paul that results in God's just condemnation (Rom 1.29–31; 2.2). Righteousness is a general moral property that entails faithfulness, since to break one's word is wrong, but is not reducible to it. Moreover, reducing God's righteousness to His covenant faithfulness makes no sense of God's relations to Gentiles, since they stand outside the covenant made with Israel. If unrighteousness is unfaithfulness to the covenant, then Gentiles cannot be said to be unrighteous, which is expressly said by Paul. Nor could a Gentile like Job be said to be righteous, since he was not faithful to the covenant.

Fortunately, proponents of the new perspective have backed away from such an overly simplistic reductionism. For example, J. D. G. Dunn, in response to his critics, acknowledges that the Hebrew concept of righteousness cannot be reduced to covenant faithfulness or salvation. Righteousness language in the Hebrew Scriptures also involves punitive divine justice, according to which righteousness is "understood as measured by a norm, right order, or that which is morally right," with the qualification that "the norm is not seen as some abstract ideal . . . but rather as a norm concretised in relation" between God and creatures (Dunn 2008, pp. 63–64). So, when we come to Romans, "That God's righteousness towards the peoples he has created includes wrath and judgment as well as faithfulness and salvation is clearly implicit in the sequences Rom. 1.16–18 and 3.3–6" (Dunn 2008, pp. 64–65). Those who deny that *dikaiosynē* is a forensic term pay insufficient attention to Rom 4.4–5, "where the forensic background is clear in the allusion to the legal impropriety of a judge 'justifying the ungodly' … and where again the thought is entirely of attributing a righteous status to one who is unrighteous" (Dunn 2008, p. 64).

1.3.2.1.3 Divine Forbearance

Having said that God put Christ forward as a sacrifice of atonement (*hilastērion*), Paul claims that God did this to show His justice, since He had passed over the sins of previous generations, the point being, presumably, that God's failure to punish previous sins allowed His justice to be called into question (cf. 2.4). But now, through Christ's sacrificial death, God's justice has been vindicated. How so? The almost inescapable implication is that these sins have now received their due; no longer can they be considered overlooked or unpunished. Punitive justice, God's justice, has been discharged in Christ. Some commentators have attempted to resist this implication by taking Paul to be saying that God demonstrates His covenant faithfulness by overlooking former sins. Not only does such a reading depend on the untenable new perspective reductionism, but *dia* + the accusative does not mean "by" but "because of," and it seems a non sequitur to say that because He had overlooked previous sins, God now puts forth Christ as a sacrificial offering as a demonstration of His faithfulness. The implication, rather, is that Christ has borne the punishment due for those sins and thereby exonerated God's justice. This understanding is confirmed by Gal 3.13, where Paul says that "Christ redeemed us from the curse of the law, having become a curse for us." Whereas we were accursed by God through disobedience to the law, Christ has rescued us by taking that cursedness upon himself.

1.3.2.1.4 Divine Forgiveness

Justification entails the forgiveness of sins. Paul writes:

> David speaks of the blessedness of those to whom God reckons righteous-
> ness apart from works:
>
>> 'Blessed are those whose iniquities are forgiven,
>>   and whose sins are covered;
>> blessed is the one against whom the Lord will not reckon sin.'
>>   (Rom 4.6–8)

It is noteworthy that biblically, the object of divine forgiveness is just as often said to be sins as sinners. Not only are people forgiven for their sins, but their sins are forgiven. This fact makes it evident that divine forgiveness is not (merely) a change of attitude on God's part toward sinners. Divine forgiveness has as its effect, not (merely) God's laying aside feelings of resentment or bitterness or anger (or what have you, according to one's favorite analysis of forgiveness), but rather the removal of the liability to punishment that attends sin. As a result of divine forgiveness, a person who formerly deserved punishment now no longer does. Because of the forgiveness that is to be found in Christ, one is no longer held accountable for one's sins. "There is therefore now no condemnation for those who are in Christ Jesus" (Rom 8.1). It is evident, then, that divine forgiveness is much more akin to legal pardon than to forgiveness as typically understood.

1.3.2.1.5 Reckoned Righteousness

According to Paul, the righteousness of God is given to all who believe in Jesus. In Rom 4 Paul goes on to explain that this gift is accorded by means of "reckoning," in the sense in which a merchant would settle accounts. Although it is sometimes said that justification involves merely acquittal and not a positive ascription of righteousness, nothing in the text warrants so diluting the righteousness of God that is reckoned to us. Biblically, the righteousness of God is a rich, variegated property, not a bare absence of guilt. Prima facie God's righteousness in its full moral rectitude is reckoned to believers (cf. Philip 3.6–9). This seems clearly expressed in II Cor 5.21: "For our sake he made him to be sin who knew no sin, so that in him we might become the righteousness of God." There is no exegetical warrant for diluting this statement: our sin is credited to Christ's account and God's righteousness is credited ours.

1.4 Representation

The promise of God's righteousness is to those who are "in Christ." This brings us to another element of the NT doctrine of the atonement: Christ as our representative.

1.4.1 OT Sacrifices

Already, in some of the OT sacrifices representation is present. For while the daily sacrifices were killed by the offerer himself, on the Day of Atonement access to the Tabernacle was permitted to the high priest alone, who therefore had to act as the people's representative before God, bringing the sacrifice for them and confessing their sins over the scapegoat (Lev 16.17).

1.4.2 Christ as Our Representative

In the NT, Christ is characterized by Paul as our representative. First, there is the corporate solidarity of all mankind with Christ, who is the antitype of the first man, Adam. Paul states, "As one man's trespass led to condemnation for all men, so one man's act of righteousness leads to acquittal and life for all men. For as by one man's disobedience many were made sinners, so by one man's obedience many will be made righteous" (Rom 5.18–19). Christ's atoning sacrifice is here conceived as universal in its scope. The representative nature of Christ's death becomes clear in Paul's statement: "We are convinced that one has died for all; therefore all have died" (II Cor 5.14). Christ did not simply die in my place; rather, what my representative did I did. Christ's death was representatively our death. This is also the import of the author of Hebrews' words: "that by the grace of God he might taste death for every one" (Heb 2.9).

Second, there is the union of believers with Christ whereby they become the beneficiaries of his atoning death (Rom 6.3–11). No universalist, Paul believed that "those who receive the abundance of grace and the free gift of righteousness will reign in life through the one man Jesus Christ" (Rom 5.17). The way in which we appropriate the benefits of Christ's atoning death is by faith culminating in baptism. This section of Paul's letter is thus not really about how we are represented by Christ on the cross, but about our faith union with him as Christians. Paul says that "all of us who have been baptized into Christ Jesus were baptized into his death" (Rom 6.3); therefore, "we have died with Christ" (v 8), "crucified with him" (v 6). Similarly, by his resurrection we "have been brought from death to life" (v 13). Because of our union with him, his death and resurrection are ours as well (cf. Col 2.12). God appointed Christ as our human representative, but we benefit from his atoning death only insofar as we are "in Christ." We are in Christ through faith and baptism, by which we identify with his death and resurrection. We, in effect, accept his representation of us. Those who reject him reject his representation of them and so are not united with him.

Thus, Paul's atonement doctrine has a strong representational aspect to it. Like Adam, Christ represents every human being before God and dies for him. Additionally, those who by faith receive God's forgiveness and righteousness thereby become the actual beneficiaries of Christ's death and resurrection on their behalf.

1.5 Redemption

There are many other facets of the NT doctrine of the atonement, but space permits mention of but one more: redemption. In the ancient world, the notion of redemption had to do with the buying of prisoners of war out of captivity or of slaves out of slavery. The payment could be called a ransom. For certain OT sacrifices, a ransom might be substituted for an animal sacrifice as a means of atonement. God is called Israel's Redeemer, though as God He need not pay a ransom to liberate people. God's great redemptive act in the OT is the Exodus signaled by the Passover.

As we have seen, Jesus described his mission as giving his life as "a ransom for many" (Mk 10.45). His life served as a payment for our liberation from sin's captivity. Similarly, NT authors did not think of our redemption as costless: "you were ransomed ... with the precious blood of Christ, like that of a lamb without blemish" (I Pet 1.17–18); "In him we have redemption through his blood" (Eph 1.7); Christ offered "his own blood, thus securing an eternal redemption" (Heb 9.12). Paul could therefore remind the Corinthians, "You were bought with a price" (I Cor 6.20).

The author of Hebrews echoes Jesus's words at the Last Supper in seeing his redemptive death as inaugurating a new covenant and forgiveness of sins: "He is the mediator of a new covenant ... since a death has occurred which redeems them from the transgressions under the first covenant" (Heb 9.15). John describes his vision of worship of the exalted sacrificial lamb:

> You are worthy to take the scroll
>   and to open its seals,
> for you were slaughtered and by your blood you ransomed for God
>   saints from every tribe and language and people and nation;
> you have made them to be a kingdom and priests serving our God,
>   and they will reign on earth.
>
> (Rev 5.9–10)

Thus is fulfilled the frustrated intention of the old covenant: "you shall be for me a priestly kingdom and a holy nation" (Exod 19.6).

1.6 Concluding Remarks

Any adequate theory of the atonement, if it is to commend itself as a Christian atonement theory, must make peace with the biblical data we have reviewed. As we turn to survey the history of dogma regarding the doctrine of the atonement, we therefore do well to keep in mind Farmer's comment: "Some exegetes appear to ... think of Christian doctrine as having come into being largely through church councils later in the history of the church. The truth is that Christian doctrine begins with biblical texts and with the earliest interpretations of those texts, which we find in the New Testament itself" (Farmer 1998, p. 275).

2 Dogmatic History of the Doctrine of the Atonement

Embroiled as they were in debates concerning the *person* of Christ, the Church Fathers devoted little time to reflection upon what later theologians were to call the *work* of Christ (e.g., his achieving atonement). No ecumenical council ever pronounced on the subject of the atonement, leaving the Church without conciliar guidance. When the Church Fathers did mention the atonement, their comments were brief and for the most part unincisive.

The remarks of the Fathers on the atonement tend to reflect the multiplicity and diversity of the NT motifs that they had inherited from the biblical authors (Mitros 1967). Eusebius, for example, wrote:

> The Lamb of God . . . was chastised on our behalf, and suffered a penalty He did not owe, but which we owed because of the multitude of our sins; and so He became the cause of the forgiveness of our sins, because He received death for us, and transferred to Himself the scourging, the insults, and the dishonour, which were due to us, and drew down on Himself the apportioned curse, being made a curse for us. And what is that but the price of our souls? And so the oracle says in our person: "By his stripes we were healed," and "The Lord delivered him for our sins." (*Demonstration of the Gospel* 10.1)

Echoing Isaiah 53 and Gal 3.13, Eusebius employs the motifs of sacrifice, vicarious suffering, penal substitution, satisfaction of divine justice, and ransom price. Similar sentiments were expressed by Origen, Cyril of Jerusalem, John Chrysostom, Cyril of Alexandria, and others (Rivière 1909).

At the same time, the Fathers portrayed Christ's death as a tremendous victory won over Satan, a view of the atonement that has come to be known as the *Christus Victor* theory (Aulén 1969). Modern scholars have tended to focus on this facet of the Fathers' teaching, doubtless because of its peculiarity and curiosity.

2.1 *Christus Victor* Theory

The so-called *Christus Victor* theory of the atonement persisted for about 900 years, from Irenaeus and Origen until the time of Anselm. According to this viewpoint, the sacrifice of Christ's life served to deliver mankind from bondage to Satan and from the corruption and death that are the consequences of sin. The Fathers sometimes interpreted Jesus's ransom saying very literally to mean that Christ's life was a payment in exchange for which human beings were set free from bondage. Such an interpretation naturally raised the question as to whom the ransom was paid. The obvious answer was the devil, since it was he who held men in bondage (II Tim 2.26; I Jn 5.19). God agreed to give His Son over to Satan's power in exchange for the human beings he held captive.

Origen, for example, asked,

> But to whom did Christ give his soul for ransom? Surely not to God. Could it then be to the Evil One? For he had us in his power until the ransom for us should be given to him, even the life of Christ. The Evil One had been deceived and led to suppose that he was capable of mastering the soul and did not see that to hold him involved a trial of strength greater than he could successfully undertake .... Hence it was not with gold or with perishable money that we were redeemed, but with the precious blood of Christ. (*Commentary on Matthew* xvi.8)

Typically, this arrangement between God and Satan was thought to be a clever trick on God's part. As the second person of the Trinity, the Son could not possibly be held captive by Satan. But by his incarnation the Son appeared weak and vulnerable like any other human being under Satan's sway. Only after the captives had been freed did the Son manifest his divine power by rising from the dead, breaking the bonds of death and hell, and escaping from Satan's power. Gregory of Nyssa offered a popular illustration of God's clever deception of Satan: "In order to secure that the ransom in our behalf might be easily accepted by him who required it, the Deity was hidden under the veil of our nature, that so, as with ravenous fish, the hook of the Deity might be gulped down along with the bait of flesh" (*Catechetical Oration* 24).

But not everyone agreed with Origen's ransom model. Gregory Nazianzus, for example, sharply denounced the ransom model for making Satan the object of Christ's atoning death (*Oration* 45.22). A different version of the *Christus Victor* theory emerged, especially among the Latin Fathers, according to which Christ was not given as a ransom to Satan but rather was the victim of Satan's deadly attack. Often confused with the ransom model, this so-called political model of *Christus Victor* attributes Satan's undoing to an overreach of authority on the devil's part. As on the ransom model, Satan was conceived to have, by God's permission, right of bondage over sinners. Thinking Christ to be vulnerable human flesh, Satan attacked and killed Christ. But unlike the sinners under Satan's authority, Christ was entirely guiltless and therefore undeserving of death. Satan had thus overstepped his authority in claiming Christ, so that God was justified in liberating those held captive by him (Augustine *On the Trinity* 4.13.17).

One of the most interesting features of the *Christus Victor* theory espoused by the Church Fathers is their widespread conviction that Christ's incarnation and death were not necessary for man's redemption. Augustine asserted bluntly: "They are fools who say the wisdom of God could not otherwise free men than by taking human nature, and being born of a woman, and suffering all that he did at the hands of sinners" (*De agone Christiano* xi). Given His omnipotence, God could have freed people from Satan's power directly. But the Fathers often emphasized God's desire to triumph over Satan, not by sheer power alone, but by just means that respected Satan's "rights." The entire arrangement was freely chosen by God as most fitting.

George Smeaton suggests that because the Church Fathers focused on the consequences of sin – principally death – rather than sin itself, they held that God in His omnipotence could redeem us without atonement. Christ's death was not required to satisfy God's justice. "They separated God's free-will from the moral perfections of His nature – rectitude, wisdom, and goodness" (Smeaton 1957, p. 509). They held that God freely chose to take on human nature in Christ as an appropriate way to deal with human mortality and death. Indeed, when concerns of justice did come into play, it was often the devil's rights that were in the forefront, not God's retributive justice.

2.2 Satisfaction Theory

Anselm's *Cur Deus homo* (*Why God Became Man*) (1098) was the first systematic exploration of the doctrine of the atonement, a work of unsurpassed importance in the history of the doctrine and a watershed between the patristic and medieval periods. Although Anselm's comprehensive atonement theory incorporates major elements of the *Christus Victor* theory, including God's victory over Satan and even a rationale for His not achieving this directly (I.23 and II.19), the fundamental thrust of Anselm's theory is very different.

Anselm's main complaint about the *Christus Victor* theory is that it is inadequate on its own to explain why God would take the extraordinary step of sending His Son to suffer and die in order to redeem mankind. In contrast to *Christus Victor* theorists, Anselm argues that the salvation of mankind is about much more than defeating Satan. It is about making satisfaction to God for man's sins. And that necessitated the incarnation and suffering of Christ.

Unfortunately, Anselm's satisfaction theory is often misrepresented in the secondary literature. It is typically said that Anselm's fundamental concern is the restoration of God's honor, which has been besmirched by man's sin. Anselm is said to portray God as a sort of feudal monarch, whose wounded ego demands some satisfaction before the insult is forgiven. Since God would be all the greater if He magnanimously forgave the insult without demanding satisfaction, Anselm's theory fails to show that Christ's atoning death was necessary.

However, a careful reading of Anselm reveals that his fundamental concern is with God's justice and its moral demands. Sin is materially bringing dishonor to God, but the reason God cannot just overlook the offense is that it would be unjust to do so and thus would contradict God's very nature.

Anselm defines sin as the failure to render to God His due. What is God's due? It is that "every wish of a rational creature should be subject to the will of God." Anselm says: "This is justice, or uprightness of will, which makes a being just or upright in heart, that is, in will; and this is the sole and complete debt of honor which we owe to God, and which God requires of us." So the honor we owe to God is to be just or upright in will. "He who does not render this honor which is due to God, robs God of his own and dishonors him; and this is sin" (I.11).

So, given the moral character of dishonoring God, Anselm asks "whether it were proper for God to put away sins by compassion alone, without any payment of the honor taken from him?" Anselm responds negatively: "To remit sin in this manner is nothing else than not to punish; and since it is not right [*recte*] to cancel sin without compensation or punishment; if it be not punished, then it is passed by undischarged" (I.12). The concern here is not merely with propriety but with its being wrong to leave sin unpunished. The concern is justice. "Truly such compassion on the part of God is wholly contrary to the Divine justice, which allows nothing but punishment as the recompense of sin" (I.24). The fundamental problem, then, is not honor but justice. Anselm's primary concern, then, is ethical and not merely with insulted dignity.

It is intriguing that Anselm sees the relevance of a Divine Command Theory of ethics to his concern with justice. For on a Divine Command Theory, God does not have any duties to fulfill, since duties are constituted by divine imperatives, and God, presumably, does not issue commands to Himself. But if God is not bound by any moral duties, it makes no sense to speak of His acting unjustly. So, Anselm asks, since God is subject to no law and His will determines what is right, why does He, being supremely merciful, not just ignore the injury done to Him (I.12)? In reply, Anselm gives the correct response to the Euthyphro Dilemma: "There is nothing more just than supreme justice, which . . . is nothing else but God himself" (I.13). God is not at liberty to do "anything improper for the Divine character." Since "the nature of God" sets limits to divine liberty, "it does not belong to his liberty or compassion or will to let the sinner go unpunished" (I.12). "Therefore, as God cannot be inconsistent with himself, his compassion cannot be of this nature" (I.24). The character or nature of God Himself necessitates that He punish sin.

Anselm allows, in fact, two ways of meeting the demands of God's justice: punishment or compensation (*satisfactio*). Anselm thus presents the atonement theorist with a choice: since the demands of divine justice must be met, there must be either punishment of or compensation for sin. Anselm chose the second alternative, since he naturally assumed that punishment would result in mankind's eternal damnation. By contrast, the later Protestant Reformers chose the first alternative, holding that Christ bore the punishment we deserved. Anselm and the Reformers are therefore very much on the same footing: In order for salvation to be possible, divine justice must somehow be satisfied.

Anselm defines compensation or satisfaction as "voluntary payment of the debt" (I.19). The difficulty we face in paying our debt, he explains, is that there is nothing we can give to God by way of compensation for our sin, since we already owe Him total obedience. Our situation is compounded by the fact that in order to compensate God, we need to give back more than we owed originally and by the gravity of our offense, having dishonored God, so that the debt we have incurred is of infinite proportion. So, no one but God could pay a debt of such magnitude, but no one but man is obliged to pay it. It follows that our salvation requires that God become man. "If it be necessary, therefore ... that the heavenly kingdom be made up of men, and this cannot be effected unless the aforesaid satisfaction be made, which none but God can make and none but man ought to make, it is necessary for the God-man to make it" (II.6).

Anselm affirms that in the incarnation of the second person of the Trinity, two complete natures are united in one person (II.7). The gift that the incarnate Christ presents to God can be found in nothing other than himself, and so he must give himself to God. Since Christ was sinless, he was under no obligation to die. By voluntarily laying down his life, he gives to God a gift of infinite value that he did not owe (II.11). On Anselm's view, Christ does not die in our place or pay the penalty for our sins; rather, he offers a compensation to God on our behalf. When Anselm affirms that Christ "allowed himself to be slain for the sake of justice" (II.18b), one must keep in mind that the demands of justice can be satisfied by either punishment or compensation. Christ offers compensation.

How, then, does the gift of Christ's life win our salvation? Anselm says that divine justice requires God the Father to reward the Son for the gift of his life. But how can a reward be bestowed on someone who needs nothing and owes nothing? The Son therefore gives the reward to those for whose salvation he became incarnate. He remits the debt incurred by their sins and bestows on them the beatitude they had forfeited (II.19). Anselm suggests that we become the beneficiaries of Christ's reward through "faith in the Gospel" and by making the Son an offering for ourselves with the love that he deserves (II.20).

2.3 Moral Influence Theory

The twelfth century logician Peter Abelard is the theologian usually associated with the moral influence theory of the atonement. According to theories of this type, Christ's death achieved our reconciliation with God, not by satisfying divine justice or ransoming us from the devil, but by moving our hearts to contrition and love as we contemplate Christ's voluntarily embracing horrible suffering and death. Nothing actually transpired between God and man at Jesus's crucifixion. No sins were punished, no debt paid. The entire power of the cross to make atonement lies in its exemplary force to produce a subjective impact in us.

In his comments on Rom 3.24–26, Abelard seeks to explain how Christ's death achieves atonement. He follows Anselm in rejecting the *Christus Victor* theory on the grounds that Satan has no right over human beings that God must respect. This raises the question, "What need was there, I say, for the Son of God, for the sake of our redemption, when he received flesh to endure so many great fasts, reproaches, lashings, spitting, and finally the most violent and shameful death of the cross?" (*Commentary on Paul's Epistle to the Romans*, Bk. 2). This is the same question that drove Anselm's inquiry. But Abelard does not seem to be persuaded by Anselm's answer that Christ's death is a compensatory gift to God. He exclaims, "How very cruel and unjust it seems that someone should require the blood of an innocent person as a ransom, or that in any way it might please him that an innocent person be slain, still less that God should have so accepted the death of his Son that through it he was reconciled to the whole world!" (Ibid.)

Anselm had met this same objection by insisting that "God the Father . . . did not compel him to suffer death, nor even allow him to be slain against his will, but of his own accord he endured death for the salvation of man" (*Cur Deus homo* I.8). Anselm's reply corrects the misimpression that God demanded the blood of an innocent person, but it remains the case that on the satisfaction theory God is pleased with the Son's free gift of his life and so is reconciled to the world.

Abelard's answer to the objection is quite different. He says:

> Nevertheless it seems to us that in this we are justified in the blood of Christ and reconciled to God, that it was through this matchless grace shown to us that his Son received our nature, and in that nature, teaching us both by word and by example, persevered to the death and bound us to himself even more

> through love, so that when we have been kindled by so great a benefit of
> divine grace, true charity might fear to endure nothing for his sake.
> (*Commentary on Paul's Epistle to the Romans*, Bk. 2)

Here Abelard seems to suggest that atonement is accomplished by Christ's igniting in us a flame of love by means of his teaching and example, persevering even unto death. Abelard even suggests that persons prior to Christ's advent were similarly moved by looking forward to the manifestation of God's love in Christ. He concludes, "Therefore, our redemption is that supreme love in us through the Passion of Christ, which not only frees us from slavery to sin, but gains for us the true liberty of the sons of God, so that we may complete all things by his love rather than by fear (Ibid., bk. 2).

Noteworthy is the fact that whereas the objectionable view was that God needed to be reconciled to the world by Christ's death, Abelard's view is that we need to be reconciled to God by Christ's death. It has become almost an axiom among modern moral influence theorists that God does not need to be reconciled to sinners; the entire obstacle lies on our side. Our hearts need to be changed so that our hostility to God evaporates and we embrace His love. So Abelard sees atonement achieved as Christ's passion enkindles our hearts and inspires love for God within us. We are liberated from sin as we come to love God more and so become more righteous.

Now taken in isolation, the moral influence theory might seem far too thin an account to do justice to the NT data concerning God's wrath, Christ's substitutionary death, justification, and so on. It seems to amount to little more than moral self-improvement inspired by Christ's example. However, scholars have recently called into question the assumption that the above, oft-quoted passage from Abelard's commentary represents Abelard's full atonement theory rather than one facet of it. In his comment on Rom 4.25 Abelard writes:

> He is said to have died **on account of our transgressions** in two ways: at one time because we transgressed, on account of which he died, and we committed sin, the penalty of which he bore; at another, that he might take away our sins by dying, that is, he swept away the penalty for sins by the price of his death, leading us into paradise, and through the demonstration of so much grace . . . he drew back our souls from the will to sin and kindled the highest love of himself. (Ibid., Bk. 2)

In this passage, Abelard appears to endorse the theory of penal substitution later expounded at length by the Protestant Reformers. Abelard affirms that Christ bore the punishment for our sins, thereby removing the punishment from us. The moral influence of Christ's death mentioned in the final clause of the sentence is now seen to be but a part of a more comprehensive theory – just as it was for Anselm, who also speaks of the influence of Christ's example of voluntary suffering (*Cur Deus homo?* II.11, 18b).

As one facet of a more complex, multifaceted theory, the moral influence theory makes a valuable contribution to understanding how the benefits won by Christ's death come to be appropriated.

2.4 Penal Substitution Theory

2.4.1 The Reformers' Doctrine

The Protestant Reformers, while appreciative of Anselm's satisfaction theory and recognizing Christ's death as satisfying God's justice, interpreted the satisfaction of God's justice in terms of penal substitution. That is to say, Christ voluntarily bore the suffering that we were due as the punishment for our sins. There is therefore no longer any punishment due to those who are the beneficiaries of Christ's death. God's wrath is propitiated by Christ's substitutionary death, for the demands of divine justice have been met.

More than that, our sins themselves having been imputed to Christ, our sin is expiated by Christ's substitutionary death. Although the imputation of our sin to Christ is purely forensic, Martin Luther could speak of it in very colorful terms:

> Being the unspotted Lamb of God, Christ was personally innocent. But because He took the sins of the world His sinlessness was defiled with the sinfulness of the world. Whatever sins I, you, all of us have committed or shall commit, they are Christ's sins as if He had committed them Himself. Our sins have to be Christ's sins or we shall perish forever ... Our merciful Father in heaven ... therefore sent His only Son into the world and said to Him: "You are now Peter, the liar; Paul, the persecutor; David, the adulterer; Adam, the disobedient; the thief on the cross. You, My Son, must pay the world's iniquity." The Law growls: "All right. If Your Son is taking the sin of the world, I see no sins anywhere else but in Him. He shall die on the Cross." And the Law kills Christ. But we go free. (Luther 1939, pp. 63–64)[9]

Moreover, just as our sins are imputed to Christ, his righteousness is imputed to us through faith in him. Luther writes, "Believe in Christ and your sins will be pardoned. His righteousness will become your righteousness, and your sins will become His sins" (1939, pp. 54–55).

2.4.2 Socinus's Critique

The Reformers' theory of penal substitution came under severe criticism by the Unitarian theologian Faustus Socinus in his *On Jesus Christ Our Savior* (1578).

---

[9] See the similar, if less colorfully expressed, views of the great French Swiss Reformer John Calvin, *Institutes of the Christian Religion* II.16.2.

In part I of this work, Socinus lays out his own atonement theory. Socinus reveals himself to be an advocate of a genuine moral influence theory, one which does not require the deity of Christ, which he denies. While Socinus's own atonement theory is today of only historical interest, his attack on penal substitution remains remarkably contemporary. In part II of his treatise, he deals extensively with the alleged exegetical basis for satisfaction and penal substitution theories. In part III, which will be the focus of our attention, he presents philosophical objections to such theories. He argues that it was neither necessary nor even possible for Christ to make satisfaction for our sins to divine justice. We shall consider his principal arguments only.

Socinus assails the contention that satisfaction of divine justice is a necessary condition of the remission of sins (Gomes 1990, III.1). He asserts that we must not think of God as a Judge "who acts according to an external legal authority and who may not deviate from the letter of the law." Rather, God should be considered a "Lord and Ruler" (*dominus et princeps*), whose will alone is "the law in everything and is the absolutely perfect standard." Anselm would, of course, have agreed but insisted that justice is essential to God's nature. Socinus, however, replies that punitive justice (or vengeance) is not an essential property of God, any more than is His mercy. If punitive justice were an attribute of God, then God could under no circumstances forgive sins; likewise, were mercy a divine attribute, God could under no circumstances punish sins. Rather, what is essential to God is His uprightness (*rectitudo*) or fairness (*aequitas*). But whether He punishes sin is up to His free will. Similarly, mercy (*misericordia*) is an essential property of God only in the sense that God is loving. But whether God chooses to pardon sinners is up to His free will.

In the next chapter, Socinus proceeds to argue that satisfaction is actually logically incompatible with the remission of sins (Gomes 1990, III.2). Remission, by definition, entails that the creditor forgoes satisfaction of the debt and that the debtor is forgiven of his obligation. If the satisfaction theorist answers that satisfaction of the debt can be made by one person and remission be given to another, Socinus will reply that because satisfaction has been made, nothing is remitted to the debtor. "There is no need for remission – indeed, remission is an impossibility – where the debt no longer exists." So it is an impossibility that a debt be both satisfied and remitted at the same time.

Socinus then presses an objection against penal substitution: a bodily punishment like eternal death cannot be endured by anyone other than the sinner himself (Gomes 1990, III.3). Admittedly, monetary penalties can be assumed legally by another person, since one person's money is just as effective as another's. But to release the guilty and to punish the innocent in their place "is not only completely opposed to any standard of justice: it is worse than inhuman and savage." If God wanted to punish our sins, then to demand the penalties from someone other than us would be contrary to justice properly so-called, namely, to uprightness and fairness, which are essential to His nature. Socinus later acknowledges that there are circumstances in which an innocent person can be afflicted without being wronged. For example, the innocent person could be under the authority of another who wishes to afflict him in order to achieve a higher purpose. "But," Socinus insists, "such affliction should not at all be regarded as penalty or punishment" (Gomes 1990, III.10).

In the case of Christ, from Socinus's Unitarian perspective, God did "not take violent action against himself: he harmed an innocent man instead" (Gomes 1990, III.3). Moreover, this innocent man was not "associated with the guilty in such a way that the guilty can be said to have undergone those penalties." Christ had "no other connection" with other human beings "except that this person, like them, is a human being." This remark raises the question whether Socinus's objections to substitutionary punishment would fail if Christ were taken to represent sinners in some way.

Socinus later asserts that it is "ridiculous and wicked" to claim that the sins of others could be imputed to an innocent person (Gomes 1990, III.10). He concedes that the sins of others can be imputed to someone, but only if (i) that person is connected to those persons in such a way that he should appear to partake of their transgressions solely because of that connection and (ii) that person has also sinned and imitated the wickedness of the others. He thinks neither condition is met in Christ's case.

Finally, Socinus argues that even if Christ's rendering satisfaction for our sins was possible, he did not in fact do so (Gomes 1990, III.4). For the penalty each of us faces is eternal death, but Christ did not literally endure this. If the penal substitution theorist says that the dignity of Christ's divine person makes his sufferings of higher value, Socinus will reply that he "would regard as unjust a law that avenges the same crime more lightly on an eminent person than it does on a common one." If it be said that God reckons the light punishments of Christ as equivalent to the punishments due us, Socinus will respond that if that be true, then Christ need not have suffered such bitter tortures and so horrible a death. "God could have made full satisfaction to his justice by exacting some extremely light penalty from Christ."

The only basis on which one could legitimately ascribe infinite value to Christ's sufferings, Socinus grants, would be that Christ is eternal God. But the divine nature is impassible, so that Christ could not have suffered in any way. Moreover, even if Christ could have suffered in his divine person, his sufferings were transitory and therefore not of infinite value. Again, even if

Christ's sufferings were of infinite value, they would have sufficed to satisfy the debt of one person alone, for we each face infinite sufferings for our sins. If one rejoins that Christ's suffering encompasses all of these infinities of punishment, then any suffering at all on his part should have sufficed to satisfy God's justice. Instead, He chose to inflict a horrible and accursed death on him.

Socinus's broadside against penal substitution elicited a flood of responses from Protestant thinkers in defense of their theory. Among the many who sought to defend the theory, the Swiss Reformed theologian Francis Turretin stands out as one of the most important.

2.4.3 Turretin's Defense

Turretin's *Institutes of Elenctic Theology* (1685) is his systematic exposition of Reformed doctrine in conversation with opposing views. In questions 10–14 of topic 14 "The Mediatorial Office of Christ," he treats the doctrine of the atonement. As with Socinus, we shall pass over Turretin's extensive survey of the exegetical basis for his claim that Christ satisfied God's justice by being substituted in our place and suffering the punishment due to us.

The foundations of Turretin's atonement doctrine are laid in his treatment of divine justice (Turretin 1992, 3.19). In contrast to Socinus, Turretin holds that punitive justice is essential to God. There are two principal virtues of God: justice and goodness. While goodness "is that by which he is conceived as the supreme good and the giver of all good," justice is "that by which God is in himself holy and just and has the constant will of giving to each his due." Although "justice" can be used as a universal term comprising all God's virtues, justice in a particular sense "gives to each his due and is occupied with the distribution of rewards and punishments and is called distributive justice." Distributive justice may be either punitive (inflicting punishment) or premiative (bestowing rewards). God's right to punish may be said to be either supreme and rigorous (called accurate right) or to be tempered by a certain moderation. The former is exercised when God imposes punishment not only on sin but also on the very person of the sinner. The latter is exercised when God grants a moderation in the imposition of punishment in time (by delaying it) or in person (by transferring it) or in degree (by mitigating it). Justice demands necessarily that all sin should be punished but does not equally demand that it should be punished in the very person sinning or at a certain time and in a certain degree.

Turretin takes cognizance of Socinus's claim that punitive justice is merely the result of God's free will. Turretin acknowledges a diversity of opinion among Christian theologians with respect to whether God must exercise punitive justice and, hence, a diversity of views concerning the necessity of satisfaction with respect to the remission of sins. In support of his view that God must exercise punitive justice, Turretin offers four arguments: (1) Scripture teaches that God detests sin and is a just Judge; (2) conscience and the consent of nations testify to the necessity of punishment for evil; (3) if sins could be expiated merely by God's will, then it is not true that it is impossible that the blood of goats and bulls should take away sin; (4) apart from the necessity of satisfaction no lawful reason could be devised for God's subjecting His Son to such an accursed and cruel death (cf. Turretin 1992, 14.10). So on Turretin's view, retributive justice, broadly conceived, is essential to God, but its exercise requires the determination of God's free will as to the time, the degree, and the persons upon whom it is inflicted.

It is also worth noting that Turretin holds to a sort of Divine Command Theory of ethics, according to which God is not bound by some external natural law. Rather, natural law is founded on God, the supreme lawgiver. The natural law is not arbitrary because God's commands are founded on the very holiness and wisdom of God Himself (1992, 11.1).

Turning to the doctrine of the atonement, Turretin explains that sin may be regarded as (i) a debt that we owe to divine justice or (ii) a mutual enmity between us and God or (iii) a crime for which we deserve everlasting death before God, the supreme ruler and judge of the world (1992, 14.10). Satisfaction for sin must therefore involve (i) payment of the debt; (ii) appeasement of divine wrath; and (iii) expiation of our guilt. This multifaceted character of satisfaction is important because the right to punish is not the private right of a creditor, though sins are sometimes compared to debts; for sins are also crimes that cannot remain unpunished without prejudice to the laws (1992, 1.19). In the case of pecuniary debt, the creditor, upon receiving satisfaction, is not said to act with indulgence because he is paid exactly what was due to him. But in a penal or criminal debt, the act of a judge is required if the guilty person is to be freed without strict enforcement of the law. This judicial act is known as *relaxation*. In such a case the very thing that is owed is not paid (namely, the criminal's undergoing punishment), but in the judge's forbearance something else is allowed.

So with respect to our sin, God can be regarded as (i) the creditor or (ii) the offended party or (iii) the judge. The "capital error" of Socinus is neglecting the last role. God "has the claims not only of a creditor or Lord (which he can assert or remit at pleasure), but also the right of government and of punishment (which is natural and indispensable)." So "God can relax his right, but not absolutely. He can do it only in so far as his justice will allow (to wit, he cannot act unjustly.)" In God's role as judge a certain forbearance can be admitted, in relation to the time by the delay of punishment or in relation to the degree by mitigation of the punishment or in relation to persons by a substitution. As the supreme judge, God can exempt sinners from the due punishment and transfer it to a substitute. In the satisfaction rendered by Christ there is a relaxation of the law in God's admission and acceptance of a substitute. Christ thus plays a threefold role as well: (i) a surety who can pay the debt for us; (ii) a mediator who takes away enmity and reconciles us to God; and (iii) a priest and victim who substitutes himself in our place for a penal satisfaction.

Under what conditions can such a substitution of the innocent for the guilty be lawfully made? Necessary conditions include: (i) a common nature of sinner and substitute so that sin may be punished in the same nature which is guilty; (ii) the free consent of the substitute's will; (iii) the substitute's having power over his own life so that he may rightfully determine what is done with it; (iv) the substitute's having power to bear all the punishment due to us and take it away as much from himself as from us; (v) the substitute's sinlessness so that he need not offer satisfaction for himself. These conditions are jointly sufficient for penal substitution. Since Christ fulfilled all these conditions, it was not unjust for Christ to substitute himself for us. "For thus no injury is done to anyone," not to Christ himself, nor to God, nor to the sinner, nor to the law, nor to the government of the universe.

Against Socinus, Turretin maintains that while Christ's punishment was not infinite as to duration, still it was equivalent as to value on account of the infinite dignity of the person suffering (1992, 14.11). Christ not only suffered a violent and bitter death but was forsaken by God the Father by His withdrawing from him the beatific vision and by suspending the joy and comfort and sense and fruition of full felicity. The law required no less to answer to the demands of justice. Although a death of infinite value was due for every individual sinner, the dignity of an infinite person swallows up and absorbs all the infinities of punishment due to us. We cannot doubt the infinite value of Christ's satisfaction, for although his human nature was finite, the satisfaction is infinite, since it is relative to the person, who is the efficient cause and to whom the obedience and suffering are to be attributed (1992, 14.12).

In Turretin's view, Christ did not merely suffer the punishment due us for our sins. Our sins themselves were imputed to Christ rather than to us (1992, 14.13). In turn, Christ's righteousness was imputed to us. Justification consists in the imputation of righteousness, not merely a righteousness of innocence but a righteousness of perseverance. The remission of sins brings the righteousness of innocence by taking away the guilt of sins, but it does not therefore bring with it the righteousness of perseverance. That righteousness is won by the lifelong obedience of Christ, whereby he completely fulfilled the law. In the same way that the sins that we committed in violation of the law are imputed to Christ, so the righteous actions by which he completely fulfilled the law for us are imputed to us. By the righteousness of Christ, Turretin does not mean the essential righteousness of God (1992, 16.3). That righteousness, he believes, could not be communicated to us without our becoming God also. The righteousness of Christ imputed to us is the obedience of his life and the suffering of his death by which he answered the demands of the law. This is called the righteousness of God because it belongs to a divine person and so is of infinite value. By this righteousness is understood the entire obedience of Christ – of his life as well as of his death, active as well as passive.

Turretin emphasizes that such imputation is a purely forensic notion and does not involve either an infusion of sin into Christ or an infusion of Christ's righteousness into us (1992, 14.16). While agreeing that by the grace of Christ inherent righteousness is infused into us, Turretin insists that it plays no role in justification: "For the righteousness of Christ alone imputed to us is the foundation and meritorious cause upon which our absolutory sentence rests, so that for no other reason does God bestow the pardon of sin and the right to life than on account of the most perfect righteousness of Christ imputed to us and apprehended by faith" (1992, 16.1). Similarly, Christ was made sin for us, not inherently or subjectively (since he knew no sin), but imputatively because God imputed to him our sins (1992, 16.3).

The word "impute," explains Turretin, properly means "to hold him who has not done a thing as if he had done it," whereas "not to impute" means "to hold him who has done a thing as if he had not done it" (1992, 16.3). He distinguishes between "imputed" and "fictitious." For imputation is no less real in its own order (judicial and forensic) than infusion is in a moral or physical order. Someone legally declared debt free is really delivered from his creditor.

An intriguing but underdeveloped aspect of Turretin's atonement theory concerns our union with Christ. He states, "The curse and punishment of sin which he received upon himself in our stead secures to us blessing and righteousness with God in virtue of that most strict union between us and him by which, as our sins are imputed to him, so in turn his obedience and righteousness are imputed to us" (1992, 16.3). This relation is not one of simple substitution; there is a union here that is the basis of the imputation of our sins to Christ and his righteousness to us. According to Turretin, so long as Christ is outside of us and we are outside of Christ we can receive no benefit from his righteousness. But God has united us with Christ by means of a twofold bond, one natural (namely, communion of nature by the incarnation), the other mystical (namely, the communion of grace by Christ's mediation), in virtue of which our sins might be imputed to Christ and his righteousness imputed to us. It is evident that imputation depends upon our union with Christ. "Having been made by God a surety for us and given to us for a head, he can communicate to us his righteousness and all of his benefits." Our union with Christ is the "cause and foundation" of our sharing in all his benefits, including justification (remission of sins and adoption as sons) (1992, 16.6).

Unfortunately, Turretin has almost nothing to say by way of explanation of what this union actually is or how it comes to be. But he thinks of it as a historical event. Prior to a person's birth, his sins cannot be said to have been remitted because nonentities have no properties and, hence, no sin and guilt to be remitted (1992, 16.5). Such a person is not yet in union with Christ and so not yet justified. Justification, though eternally decreed, takes place in this life in the moment of God's effectual calling, by which the sinner is transferred from a state of sin to a state of grace and is united to Christ, his head, by faith. "For hence it is that the righteousness of Christ is imputed to him by God, by whose merit apprehended by faith he is absolved from his sins and obtains a right to life" (1992, 16.9). Faith is thus "the instrumental cause of our justification" (1992, 16.7) and by implication of our union with Christ. Hence, believers have "immediate and absolute union" with Christ (1992, 18.25).

In virtue of our union with Christ, his righteousness is imputed to us (Turretin 1992, 16.4). The imputation of his righteousness brings two benefits: the remission of sins and the bestowal of a right to life (in which two benefits the whole of justification is comprised). In Turretin's view, the imputation of righteousness is explanatorily prior to the remission of sins. If we wish to philosophize correctly, he advises, we must not say that God first remits our sins and afterward imputes Christ's righteousness to us; rather, God first imputes Christ's righteousness and afterward, on account of that imputed righteousness, remits our sins. Turretin explains that a satisfaction must necessarily intervene in order that remission may be granted by God without detriment to His justice, and that it may be the foundation of the absolving sentence.

Thus, Turretin's atonement theory has a peculiar explanatory structure: first, we are through faith united with Christ as our head by nature and by his mediatorial office; next, in virtue of our union with Christ, his righteousness is imputed to us; finally, in virtue of his imputed righteousness, our sins are remitted, since God's justice has been satisfied by Christ's vicarious suffering and death, and we are given the right to life, adoption as sons.

2.5 Governmental Theory

The final atonement theory we shall survey is the governmental theory usually associated with Hugo Grotius, a famous international jurist who published a treatise in response to Socinus on the doctrine of the atonement entitled *A Defence of the Catholic Faith Concerning the Satisfaction of Christ, against Faustus Socinus* (1617).

Unfortunately, Grotius's theory is today widely misrepresented in the secondary literature. He is even accused of capitulating to Socinus and betraying the Reformers' theory of penal substitution, offering in its place a quite different theory, which has come to be known as the governmental theory. According to this theory, as typically presented, God is to be conceived as the sovereign Ruler of the world. As such, it lies entirely within His discretion to remit sins without satisfaction. Christ was not therefore punished substitutionally for our sins. Rather, God chose to inflict terrible suffering on him as an example to us of what sin deserves, so that we shall be motivated to live holy lives before God. God's freely choosing to thus afflict Christ is done for the sake of the moral governance of the world. On this view, Grotius's theory is a combination of the moral influence theory with a consequentialist view of punishment for the sake of deterrence.

By contrast, Grotius expressly presents his treatise as a defense of penal substitution. He states:

> The catholic doctrine therefore is as follows: God was moved by his own goodness to bestow distinguished blessings upon us. But since our sins, which deserved punishment, were an obstacle to this, he determined that Christ, being willing of his own love toward men, should, by bearing the most severe tortures, and a bloody and ignominious death, pay the penalty for our sins, in order that without prejudice to the exhibition of the divine justice, we might be liberated, upon the intervention of a true faith, from the punishment of eternal death. (Grotius 1889, I)

After a fairly impressive exegesis of the biblical text in both Greek and Hebrew, Grotius concludes that Christ's death was, indeed, a punishment:

> To sum up what has been already said: since the Scripture says that Christ was chastised by God, i.e. punished; that Christ bore our sins, i.e. the punishment of sins; was made sin, i.e. was subjected to the penalty of sins; was made a curse with God, or was exposed to the curse, that is, the penalty of the law; since, moreover, the very suffering of Christ, full of tortures, bloody, ignominious, is most appropriate matter of punishment; since, again, the Scripture says that these were inflicted on him by God on account of our sins, i.e. our sins so deserving; since death itself is said to be the wages, i.e. the punishment of sin;

> certainly it can by no means be doubted that with reference to God the suffering and death of Christ had the character of a punishment. (Grotius 1889, I)

Grotius's view of divine justice is retributive and of Christ's death a punishment for our sins.

God's purpose in Christ's death was twofold: first, to demonstrate divine retributive justice with respect to sin, which had so long been postponed; second, to exempt us from punishment by remission of our sins. Grotius ridicules Socinus's moral influence theory, according to which the death of Christ is meant to persuade us to exercise faith in hope of eternal life: "What can be more widely removed from the truth, we ask, than that the death of a perfectly innocent man, so bloody, should of itself have power to persuade us that the greatest joys are prepared by God for those who live holily?" (Grotius 1889, I).

Grotius concedes to Socinus that we should not think of God as a judge placed under the law, for such a judge could not liberate the guilty from punishment (1889, II). But neither should we think of God as Socinus often does, as an offended party in a personal dispute. For such a private person has no right to punish another or even to demand punishment of another. Certainly, God is offended by sin, but He does not act as merely the offended party in punishing it. Rather, God should be considered to act as a Ruler. "For to inflict punishment, or to liberate any one from punishment ... is only the prerogative of the ruler as such, primarily and *per* se; as, for example, of a father in a family, of a king in a state, of God in the universe" (Grotius 1889, II). Grotius thinks it would be unjust in a ruler, even in God, to let certain sins go unpunished, such as sins of the unrepentant, and so it is inconsistent with the justice of God that He should remit all punishment whatsoever.

Grotius appeals to the notion of relaxation to explain God's act of punishing Christ in the place of sinners:

> The act of God of which we treat will be the punishment of one to obtain the impunity of another ... the act will be a method of relaxing or moderating the same law, which relaxation we call, in these days, dispensation. It may be defined: The act of a superior by which the obligation of an unabrogated law upon certain persons or things is removed. (Grotius 1889, III)

Although some laws are not relaxable because their opposite involves immutable wickedness, all positive laws are relaxable. Grotius thus combines a view of justice as retributive with the possibility of relaxation of the law by an authority.

> That he who has committed a crime deserves punishment and is on that account liable to punishment necessarily follows from the very relation of sin and the sinner to the superior and is properly natural. But that all sinners should be punished with a punishment corresponding to the crime is not simply and universally necessary, nor properly natural, but only harmonious with nature. Hence, it follows that nothing prevents the law which demands this from being relaxable.

So on Grotius's view, retributive justice permits but does not require punishment. God had a very weighty reason for relaxing the law so as not to punish us but Christ in our stead; namely, had He not done so, the entire human race would have been destroyed.

Imputation seems to play no role in Grotius's theory. Christ's bearing our sin is interpreted to mean that Christ bore the punishment for our sin. Justification is taken to be a declaration of innocence rather than to include the imputation of Christ's righteousness to us. On Grotius's view Christ was thus completely innocent, both personally and even legally. God chose to punish him for our sins so that our debt of punishment might be remitted and we be liberated.

Grotius next takes up three objections to substitutionary atonement (1889, IV). We shall consider the first two. First is the objection that it was unjust to punish Christ in our place. Socinus acknowledges that it was not unjust that God should afflict Christ with suffering, but he denies that such suffering could effect anything to obtain our pardon. Grotius maintains, to the contrary, that it was neither unjust nor contrary to the nature of punishment that someone should be punished for another's sins. With respect to the nature of punishment, Grotius (1889, V) makes the astute observation that "innocence does not prevent punishment any more than it does affliction" – a person might be punished *though* innocent. As to the justice of God's punishing an innocent person, Grotius maintains that Scriptural prohibitions against punishing children for the sins of their fathers is, in part, a positive law imposed by God upon humanity, but God Himself "is not bound by it, since he has never imposed it upon himself, nor indeed can he be bound by any law" (1889, V).

Socinus claims that there ought to be some connection between the guilty party and the person who is punished in his place. Grotius agrees but points out that Christ was designated by God Himself as the head of the body of which we are members. God has the right to afflict Christ, and Christ has freely assented to the same, and so nothing prevents God's ordaining that that affliction be the punishment for the sins of others connected to him.

The second objection concerns whether God had sufficient reason to punish Christ in our place (1889, V). Socinus errs in thinking that the reason for Christ's substitutionary death must show that his death was necessary. Appealing to the

Church Fathers, Grotius argues that God had good reasons for not remitting our sins without punishing Christ, though He might have done so. God was unwilling to pass over so many and such heinous sins without testifying by some act how greatly displeased He is with sin. The act most suitable for this is punishment. Moreover, to neglect to punish sin altogether leads to a lower estimation of sin, whereas, on the other hand, the best means of preventing sin is the fear of punishment. Not only so, but in Christ's voluntary self-sacrifice God declares in a marked way His great love for us. Thus, God in His most perfect wisdom chose that way of redemption by means of which He could manifest both His hatred of sin and His love of mankind.

Misrepresentations are always based upon half-truths, and so it is with Grotius's so-called governmental theory. It is true that he thought that God as Ruler could remit sins without satisfaction while preserving His essential justice and holiness. But against Socinus, Grotius thinks that God had powerful reasons, namely, setting an example for us, for a merely partial relaxation of the law, so that another might satisfy divine justice by bearing the punishment we deserved. As the supreme Ruler He had the right to do this.

> There is, therefore, no unfairness in this, that God, whose is the supreme power in respect to all things not unjust *per* se, and who is bound by no law, determined to employ the tortures and death of Christ to set forth a weighty example against the great crimes of all of us with whom Christ was very closely connected by his nature and kingdom and suretyship. (Grotius 1889, IV)

2.6 Concluding Remarks

With the Enlightenment came a proliferation of atonement theories, as theologians abandoned the traditional approaches. Not only would it be impossible to survey here the bewildering variety of atonement theories characteristic of modernity, but most of them do not represent live options for the Christian philosopher or theologian who wishes to work within biblical parameters.

3 Philosophical Reflections

We come at last to reflect philosophically upon issues raised by atonement theories. We want to explore what options are open to a biblically faithful atonement theorist. While not defending a specific atonement theory, I do think that any adequate theory must incorporate the following elements.

3.1 Penal Substitution

First, an essential – and indeed, central – facet of any biblically adequate atonement theory is penal substitution. Penal substitution in a theological context is the doctrine that God inflicted upon Christ the suffering that we deserved as the punishment for our sins, as a result of which we no longer deserve punishment. Notice that this explication leaves open the question whether Christ was punished for our sins. Some defenders of penal substitution recoil at the thought that God punished His beloved Son for our sins. Rather, God afflicted Christ with the suffering which, had it been inflicted upon us, would have been our just desert and, hence, punishment. In other words, Christ was not punished, but he endured the suffering that would have been our punishment had it been inflicted on us. We do not want to exclude by definition such accounts as being penal substitutionary theories, since Christ on such accounts suffers as our substitute and bears what would have been our punishment, thereby freeing us from punishment. Of course, this explication also permits the penal substitution theorist to affirm that Christ was, indeed, punished in our place and so bore the punishment for our sins.

No atonement theory which omits penal substitution can hope to account adequately for the biblical data we have surveyed, particularly Isaiah 53 and its NT employment. More than that, penal substitution, if true, could not be a merely tangential facet of an adequate atonement theory, for it would prove foundational to so many other aspects of the atonement, such as redemption from sin, satisfaction of divine justice, and the moral influence of Christ's example. So a multifaceted atonement theory must include penal substitution at its center.

The doctrine of penal substitution, ever since the time of Socinus, has faced formidable, and some would say insuperable, philosophical challenges. In discussing these challenges, our aim is to explore some of the various options open to the Christian thinker. A discussion of such challenges takes us into lively debates over questions in the philosophy of law, particularly questions about the theory of punishment. Unfortunately, most theologians, and in fact most Christian philosophers, have little familiarity with these debates. The doctrine of penal substitution is usually dismissed by its critics in a single paragraph, even a single sentence, to the effect that it would be unjust of God to punish an innocent person for others' sins, end of discussion. We need to go deeper.

One's theory of punishment should offer both a *definition of punishment* and a *justification of punishment*, aspects of the theory of punishment that legal philosophers have teased apart only in recent decades. A definition of punishment will enable us to determine whether some act counts as punishment, while a justification of punishment will help us to determine whether a punitive act is permitted or even required, depending on one's theory. Both of these aspects of the theory of punishment are relevant to the doctrine of penal substitution. Indeed, penal substitution is not infrequently discussed in an entirely nontheological context. It will be up to the Christian philosopher to make the theological application.

A cautionary word is, however, in order at this point. The punishment that is discussed by legal theorists and philosophers of law is almost invariably legal punishment in the context of criminal law. Even when discussing penalties that are mandated by civil law rather than criminal law, the framework is still legal. One is discussing punishment as administered by the state as part of a system of justice. While analogous to divine justice, human systems of justice will also have features that are significantly disanalogous to divine justice. To give an obvious example, the state may be forced not to administer punishment as a result of lack of prison space due to overcrowding and lack of resources. God is evidently not so hampered. Still, legal theorists and philosophers of law have poured an enormous amount of thought into the theory of punishment, and so, given the widespread presence of forensic and judicial motifs in the biblical texts pertinent to the atonement, we may expect to learn a great deal from them.

3.1.1 Definition of Punishment

What, then, is punishment? Punishment involves, first, harsh treatment, as is obvious from typical cases of punishment. Theorists prefer the term "harsh treatment" to "suffering" because the latter is subjective and, hence, person relative – the masochist might enjoy being treated harshly and so would not be "punished!" Harsh treatment is not sufficient for punishment, however. As Socinus recognized, God may inflict suffering on some person without its being punishment. So what transforms harsh treatment into punishment? This is where the debate begins.

3.1.1.1 The Alleged Incoherence of Penal Substitution

No consensus exists concerning the conditions sufficient for punishment. But consider Alec Walen's characterization of some of the necessary conditions of punishment in a standard philosophical encyclopedia:

> For an act to count as punishment, it must have four elements:
>
> First, it must impose some sort of cost or hardship on, or at the very least withdraw a benefit that would otherwise be enjoyed by, the person being punished.

Second, the punisher must do so intentionally, not as an accident, and not as a side-effect of pursuing some other end.

Third, the hardship or loss must be imposed in response to what is believed to be a wrongful act or omission.

Fourth, the hardship or loss must be imposed, at least in part, as a way of sending a message of condemnation or censure for what is believed to be a wrongful act or omission. (Walen 2014)

Most theorists would also want to require that the hardship or loss be imposed by a recognized authority, so as to distinguish punishment from personal vengeance or vigilantism.

Walen's characterization is a version of what is called an expressivist theory of punishment, made popular by Joel Feinberg, according to which the harsh treatment imposed must express condemnation or censure in order to count as punishment (Feinberg 1970). Some critics of penal substitution have claimed that given an expressivist theory of punishment, it is conceptually impossible that God punish Christ for our sins (Murphy 2009, pp. 255–59). For God could not condemn or censure Christ, since he did no wrong. The point is not that it would be immoral for God to punish Christ for others' wrongs, but that any such harsh treatment inflicted on him by God for those wrongs would not count as punishment because it would not express condemnation or censure.

The crucial premises of this argument seem to be the following:

1. If Christ was sinless, God could not have condemned Christ.
2. If God could not have condemned Christ, God could not have punished Christ.
3. If God could not have punished Christ, penal substitution is false.

Thus, it follows from the sinlessness of Christ that penal substitution is false.

3.1.1.2 Responses to the Alleged Incoherence of Penal Substitution

There are a number of ways in which the proponent of penal substitution might respond to the coherence objection.

3.1.1.2.1 Penal Substitution without Punishment

A penal substitution theorist who holds that God did not punish Christ denies premise (3) in §3.1.1.1, and so will be unfazed by and perhaps even welcome this objection. Such a theorist, if he wishes, may simply use a different word than "punishment" to characterize Christ's suffering. Feinberg, for example, distinguishes *penalties*, such as parking tickets, offside penalties in sports, firings at work, flunkings in school, and so on, from *punishments* technically so-called, which always express condemnation. Borrowing this distinction, the defender of penal substitution may say that God penalized Christ for our sins, that Christ paid the penalty for our sins. If God's harsh treatment of Christ did not express condemnation, then God did not punish Christ for our sins, but He may still be said to have penalized him for our sins. Feinberg recognizes that inflicting penalties on an innocent person may be even worse than inflicting punishments on an innocent person (Feinberg 1970, p. 112). The debate will then move on to the familiar question of the morality of afflicting an innocent person with the suffering that we deserved as the punishment for our sins.

3.1.1.2.2 Punishment without Expressivism

If the penal substitution theorist holds that God did punish Christ for our sins, then it is open to him to deny premise (2) in §3.1.1.1. He might simply reject an expressivist theory of punishment. Though popular, it is not as though the theory has overwhelming arguments in support. Indeed, one of the problems with the theory is that, contrary to claims of its proponents (Murphy 2009, p. 256), the line between punishments and mere penalties in the law does not coincide with the line between condemnatory and non-condemnatory harsh treatment.[10] Penalties can be very harsh, indeed, and plausibly often express society's "resentment" and "stern judgment of disapproval" for the wrong done.[11] This seems undeniable in cases involving torts such as assault and battery, defamation, fraud, and wrongful death. Arthur Ripstein explains that tort law articulates certain norms of acceptable conduct, and if the plaintiff is to recover damages from the defendant, he must show that the defendant has violated those norms (Ripstein 2002, p. 658). The judgment of the unacceptability of the defendant's conduct may often be so severe as to express

---

[10] Because of these ambiguities, Zaibert considers Feinberg's expressivist theory to be actually dangerous for a democratic society because what are clearly punitive measures can be rationalized by the state as mere penalties. "Pragmatically speaking, the most problematic aspect of Feinberg's view is that it opens up the possibility for the State to inflict painful treatment upon its citizens, a treatment which is 'much worse than punishment', but for which the citizens have fewer defenses than they would if they had been 'merely' punished. 'Even floggings and imposed fastings,' Feinberg continues, 'do not constitute punishments, then, where social conventions are such that they do not express public censure'" (Zaibert 2006, p. 113). The U.S. Supreme Court, Zaibert notes, has had considerable difficulty in interpreting the eighth amendment's prohibition of cruel and unusual punishment because it is unclear what actions count as punishment. One notorious example is the Court's decision in *Fleming v. Nestor* (1960) that deportation is merely an administrative matter and not punishment, despite the fact that deportation in that (and other cases) seems to be punitive (Zaibert 2006, pp. 48, 54). "The widespread standard account makes it easy for the state to abuse its punitive power by masquerading punitive measures as if they were not really punitive, labeling certain governmental acts as merely administrative, as if this label would *deus ex machina* obscure the fact that some such acts are clearly punitive" (Zaibert 2006, p. 4).

[11] The fusion of resentment and reprobation (stern disapproval) is what Feinberg calls condemnation.

condemnation. Indeed, some torts are also crimes, in which case the act for which compensatory damages are awarded is also the object of condemnation in a criminal verdict. And even for torts that are not crimes, sometimes the damages awarded are actually punitive damages, which exceed the aims of merely corrective justice. Very large awards in particular plausibly often express society's strong disapproval of the wrong done to the plaintiff. Even in sports, penalties imposed for fouls like unsportsmanlike conduct and taunting seem to carry censure with them. While these infractions are not crimes, since they are not violations of criminal law, still the penalties imposed for such infractions plausibly express condemnation.

By the same token, there are crimes that are punishable, even though such punishments do not seem to express condemnation. For example, crimes involving so-called *mala prohibita* are punishable, even though such punishments may no longer express resentment or stern disapproval, such as punishment for violation of federal laws against marijuana possession (Husak 2005, pp. 65–90). Moreover, there are in the criminal law cases of so-called strict liability in which crimes are committed without fault and yet are punishable. These cases are far from unusual, there being many thousands of statutory offenses involving elements of strict liability, including crimes like possession of narcotics or firearms and the selling of mislabeled foods or of prescription drugs without a prescription (Ormerod 2011, ch. 7). Punishments for crimes of strict liability often seem to involve no condemnation of the person involved and yet are still punishments in our criminal justice system.

In fact, penal substitution in a secular context furnishes a powerful counterexample to the claim that punishment inherently expresses an attitude of censure or condemnation toward the person punished. As Grotius documents (1889, IV), the punishment of a substitute was well understood and widely accepted in the ancient world,[12] and those who voluntarily stepped forward to die as a substitute for someone else were universally admired as paradigms of nobility. We moderns may regard such a practice as immoral and ourselves as more enlightened for renouncing it, but it would be an example of cultural imperialism to claim that these ancient societies did not really endorse and even practice substitutionary punishment. To think that because it was unjust it was not punishment is to confuse the definition of punishment with the justification of punishment, an error made by theorists who similarly held that punishment

---

[12] See further Gathercole (2015, ch. 3). According to Gathercole, the preeminent example of substitutionary death in classical literature is Euripides' Alcestis, who was willing to die in place of her husband Admetus. In Rom 5.7–8 Paul compares the death of Jesus with other heroic deaths that his Roman readers might have known. Gathercole thinks that Alcestis may well be the example that Paul had in mind.

of the innocent is not really punishment. Just as most theorists today recognize that it is possible to punish the innocent, so we should acknowledge the possibility of punishing a substitute.

3.1.1.2.3 Expressivism without Condemnation of Christ

But the penal substitution theorist need not reject expressivism outright in order to deny premise (2) in §3.1.1.1. For expressivism as typically formulated is wholly consistent with penal substitution. Consider, once again, Walen's account. His fourth condition does not require that the person punished is condemned or censured for the act or omission believed to be wrong. Censure could be either of the person who did the act or of the act itself. Similarly, on Feinberg's account "punishment expresses the community's strong disapproval of *what the criminal did*. Indeed it can be said that punishment expresses the judgment of the community that *what the criminal did* was wrong" (Feinberg 1970, p. 100 [my emphasis]).[13] Even if we say that punishment expresses condemnation of the wrongdoer as the performer of the wrong,[14] we have not ruled out penal substitution, for we have not required that condemnation be directed toward the person bearing the punishment.

In fact, it needs to be asked whether critics of the coherence of penal substitution have not fundamentally misunderstood expressivism with regard to punishment. Expressivism holds that there is a certain stigma attached to punishment, in the absence of which the harsh treatment is not punishment. It is no part of expressivism that the censure expressed by punishment target a particular person. Expressivist theories of punishment, as typically formulated, are perfectly consistent with penal substitution – which is just as it should be, given the attitudes of those in societies endorsing or practicing penal substitution. Hence, premise (2) in §3.1.1.1 is undercut.

3.1.1.2.4 Condemnation of Christ without Personal Sin and Guilt

But suppose one adopts an expressivist theory of punishment that does require that condemnation be directed toward the person punished. Would such a theory rule out penal substitution? Not necessarily, for one might espouse a theory of penal substitution that includes the imputation of sin, such as the Reformers articulated and Turretin defended. On such a theory, Christ, though personally without moral fault, is legally guilty and so condemned

---

[13] An even stronger attitude or judgment of condemnation may be directed as well toward *what the criminal did*.

[14] Ironically, Murphy's own formulation, intended to show the incoherence of penal substitution (2009, p. 256). Cf. critique by Hill and Jedwab (2015).

by God for our sins. Hence, premise (1) in §3.1.1.1 is denied. Critics of the coherence of penal substitution admit that given the doctrine of the imputation of sins, their charge of incoherence fails; but they reject the doctrine of imputation (Murphy 2009, p. 259).

Murphy distinguishes two possible imputation doctrines: one that holds that our sins, that is to say, our wrongful acts, were imputed to Christ, and one that holds that our guilt for our wrongful acts was imputed to Christ. Murphy's complaint in both cases is the same: we have no experience of the *transfer* either of moral responsibility for actions or of guilt in isolation from actions from one person to another.

The force of Murphy's objection depends on the probability that if the doctrine of imputation is true, then we should have some experience of such a transfer in human affairs. But why think that? The proponent of penal substitution might plausibly respond that our want of such experience is hardly surprising, since imputation of sins or guilt is a uniquely divine prerogative. Arguably, God and only God as supreme Lawgiver, Judge, and Ruler is in a position to impute the sins and guilt of one person to another. So it would be hardly surprising if imputation of sin, though a divine prerogative, failed to find an analogy in our system of justice.

3.1.1.2.4.1 Imputation of Sins and Legal Fictions

But are we so utterly bereft of analogies to imputation as Murphy alleges? I think not. Consider first the idea that our wrongful acts were imputed to Christ. On this view, although Christ did not himself commit the sins in question, God chose to treat Christ *as if* he had done those acts. Such language is formulaic for the expression of legal fictions.[15] The nearly universal understanding of a legal fiction is that it is something that the court consciously knows to be false but treats as if it were true for the sake of a particular action. The use of legal fictions is a long-established, widespread, and indispensable feature of systems of law.

Penal substitution theorists have typically been understandably leery of talk of legal fictions in connection with their views, lest our redemption be thought to be something unreal, a mere pretense. But such a fear is misplaced. The claim is not that penal substitution is a fiction, for Christ was really and truly punished on such a view. Nor is his expiation of sin or propitiation of God's wrath a fiction, for his being punished for our sins removed our liability to punishment and satisfied God's justice. All these things are real. What is fictitious is that Christ himself did the wrongful acts for which he was punished.

---

[15] The seminal treatment of contemporary discussions is Fuller (1930), (1931a), and (1931b). The more distant progenitor is Vaihinger (Vaihinger 1949).

Every orthodox Christian believes that Christ did not and could not commit sins, but on the present view, God adopts for the administration of justice the legal fiction that Christ did such deeds.

Penal substitution theorists will sometimes object to the employment of legal fictions in the doctrine of the atonement because God's legally justifying us has real, objective results. Someone whose debt has been legally remitted, for example, really becomes free of the burden of financial obligation to his former creditor. But such an objection is based on a misunderstanding of the role of legal fictions in the achievement of justice. A legal fiction is a device that is adopted precisely in order to bring about real and objective differences in the world.

Take, for example, the classic example of a legal fiction employed in *Mostyn v. Fabrigas* (1774). Mr. Fabrigas sued the governor of the Mediterranean island of Minorca, then under British control, for trespass and false imprisonment. Since such a suit could not proceed in Minorca without the approval of the governor himself, Mr. Fabrigas filed suit in the Court of Common Pleas in London. Unfortunately, that court had jurisdiction only in cases brought by residents of London. Lord Mansfield, recognizing that a denial of jurisdiction in this case would leave someone who was plainly wronged without a legal remedy, declared that for the purposes of the action Minorca was part of London! Frederick Schauer observes, "That conclusion was plainly false and equally plainly produced a just result, and thus *Mostyn v. Fabrigas* represents the paradigmatic example of using a fiction to achieve what might in earlier days have been done through the vehicle of equity" (Schauer 2015, p. 122).[16]

Or consider the legal fiction that a ship is a person.[17] The adoption of this fiction by U.S. federal courts in the early nineteenth century came about because of the efforts of ship owners to evade responsibility for violating embargo laws and carrying unlawful cargo, including slaves. When the ships were seized, the captains and crews passed on legal responsibility to the ship owners, who in turn produced innocent manifests while denying any knowledge of the illegal activity of the captains and crews. The courts responded by making the ship itself (herself?) the person against whom charges were brought. By the end of the century, this fiction became the settled view of ships in maritime law, so that the "offending ship is considered as herself the wrongdoer, and as herself bound to make compensation for the wrong done" (*The John G. Stevens* 170 U.S. 113, 122 [1898]). According to Lind, the

---

[16] By "equity," Schauer has reference to recourse to "an elaborate series of Chancellor's courts known as courts of equity, in order to gain equitable relief from the rigidity of law."

[17] Described colorfully by Lind (2015, pp. 95–96).

"ontologically wild" fiction of ship personification had profound and beneficial results, facilitating the condemnation and forfeiture of offending vessels and producing a more just, coherent, and workable admiralty jurisprudence (Lind 2015, p. 96).

Holding that God, in His role as supreme Judge, adopts for the purposes of our redemption the legal fiction that Christ himself had done the deeds in question in no way implies that our forensic justification before His bar is unreal. Thus, through the device of legal fictions we do, indeed, have some experience of how legal responsibility for acts can be imputed to another person who did not really do the actions, thereby producing real differences in the world outside the fiction.

3.1.1.2.4.2 Imputation of Guilt and Vicarious Liability

Consider now the second alternative, that God imputes to Christ, not the wrongdoing itself, but the guilt of our wrongdoing.[18] It is worth noting that the question does not, *pace* Murphy, concern the *transfer* of guilt from one person to another, in the sense that guilt is removed from one person and placed on another. For the defender of the doctrine of imputation does not hold that when my guilt is imputed to Christ, it is thereby removed from me. Guilt is merely replicated in Christ, just as, according to the doctrine of original sin, Adam's guilt was replicated in me, not transferred from Adam to me. Adam remains guilty, as do I when my guilt is imputed to Christ. The entire rationale of penal substitution is, after all, the removal of guilt by punishment.

What is at issue, then, is whether we have any experience of the *replication* of guilt in a person different than the person who did the act. The question is not the removal of the primary actor's guilt but the imputation of guilt for his wrongdoing to another as well. So understood, we are not wholly without analogies in our justice system.

In civil law there are cases involving what is called vicarious liability. In such cases the principle of *respondeat superior* is invoked in order to impute the

---

[18] What follows could have also been said with respect to the vicarious liability of corporations as persons in the eyes of the law. Ormerod explains, "Corporations have a separate legal identity. They are treated in law as having a legal personality distinct from the natural persons – members, directors, employees, etc. – who make up the corporation. That presents the opportunity, in theory, of imposing liability on the corporation separately from any criminal liability which might be imposed on the individual members for any wrongdoing" (Ormerod 2011, p. 256). But because corporate persons might be thought by some to be legal fictions, I leave them aside to focus on the vicarious liability of human beings. It is also worth noting that vicarious liability may also, via the so-called delegation principle and attributed act principle, involve the imputation of acts and not just guilt to innocent persons (Ormerod 2011, pp. 277, 279). In that case, appeal to legal fictions as an analogy to imputation of sins becomes superfluous.

liability of a subordinate to his superior, for example, a master's being held liable for acts done by his servant. On the contemporary scene this principle has given rise to a widespread and largely uncontroversial principle of vicarious liability of employers. An employer may be held liable for acts done by his employee in his role as employee, even though the employer did not do these acts himself. Cases typically involve employers' being held liable for the illegal sale of items by employees, but may also include torts like assault and battery, fraud, manslaughter, and so on.

It needs to be emphasized that the employer is not, in such cases, being held liable for other acts, such as complicity or negligence in failing to supervise the employee. Indeed, he may be utterly blameless in the matter. Rather, the liability incurred by his employee for certain acts is imputed to him in virtue of his relationship with the employee, even though he did not himself do the acts in question.[19] The liability is not thereby transferred from the employee to the employer; rather, the liability of the employee is replicated in the employer. In cases of vicarious liability, then, we have the responsibility for the act, apart from the act itself, imputed to another person than the actor.

It might be said that in such civil cases guilt is not imputed to another person, but mere liability. This claim may be left moot,[20] for vicarious liability also makes an appearance in criminal law as well as civil law.[21] There are criminal as well as civil applications of *respondeat superior*. The liability for crimes committed by a subordinate in the discharge of his duties can also be imputed to his superior. Both the employer and the employee may be found guilty for crimes that only the employee committed.[22] For example, in *Allen v. Whitehead* (1930), the owner of a café was found to be guilty because his employee, to whom management of the café had been delegated, allowed prostitutes to congregate there in violation of the law. In *Sherras v. De Rutzen* (1895), a bartender's criminal liability for selling alcohol to a constable on duty was imputed to the licensed owner of the bar. In such cases, we have the guilt of one person imputed to another person, who did not do the act. Interestingly, vicarious liability is another case of strict liability, where the superior is held to be guilty without being found blameworthy, since no *mens rea* (blameworthy

---

[19] Intriguingly, a necessary condition of vicarious liability is that the superior be so related to the subordinate as to have either the right, the power, or the duty to prevent the subordinate's wrongdoing. Christ, of course, stands in such a relationship to us, since he possesses both the power and the right to prevent our sinning, even if he has no duty to do so.

[20] See pp. 87–90.   [21] See Leigh (1982).

[22] Leigh (1982, p. 1) notes that vicarious liability takes two forms. In one, a person is held liable for the acts of another who has a *mens rea*, while in the other, more typical case, a person is held liable for the act of another where the act of the other person amounts to an offense of strict liability. For the two examples here, see Ormerod (2011, pp. 274, 277).

mental state) is required.[23] He is thus guilty and liable to punishment even though he is not culpable.

Thus, the vicarious liability that exists in the law suffices to show that the imputation of our guilt to Christ is not wholly without parallel in our experience. In the law's imputation of guilt to a person other than the actor, we actually have a very close analogy to the doctrine of the imputation of our guilt to Christ.

Much more needs to be said about the doctrine of imputation when it comes to the satisfaction of divine justice (§3.2.2.2), but for now it is sufficient that we see how such a doctrine dissolves any allegations of incoherence respecting substitution and the definition of punishment.

In summary, in response to the coherence objection, the proponent of penal substitution may either agree that Christ was not punished or else hold that an expressivist theory of punishment is either mistaken or compatible with substitutionary punishment.

3.1.2 Justification of Punishment

We now come to the more important question of what justifies the imposition of punishment. One's justification of punishment will be determined by one's overarching theory of justice. Theories of justice may be classified as broadly *retributive* or *consequentialist*. Retributive theories of justice hold that punishment is justified because the guilty deserve to be punished. Consequentialist theories of justice hold that punishment is justified because of the extrinsic goods that may be realized thereby, such as deterrence of crime, sequestration of dangerous persons, and reformation of wrongdoers. Retributive theories are often said to be retrospective, imposing punishment for crimes committed, whereas consequentialist theories are prospective, aiming to prevent crimes from being committed.

3.1.2.1 The Alleged Injustice of Penal Substitution

Critics of penal substitution frequently assert that God's punishing Christ in our place would be an injustice on God's part. For it is an axiom of retributive justice that it is unjust to punish an innocent person. But Christ was an innocent person. Since God is perfectly just, He cannot therefore have punished Christ. It does no good to say that Christ willingly undertook this

---

[23] Indeed, the superior is entirely innocent, being ascribed neither a *mens rea* nor an *actus reus* (wrongful act), but is declared guilty by imputation. Note, moreover, that in a criminal case involving vicarious liability, the punishment of the employer can satisfy for the employee as well.

self-sacrifice on our behalf, for the nobility of his selfless act does not annul
the injustice of punishing an innocent person for deeds he did not do.

The crucial premises and inferences of this objection appear to be the
following:

1. God is perfectly just.
2. If God is perfectly just, He cannot punish an innocent person.
3. Therefore, God cannot punish an innocent person.
4. Christ was an innocent person.
5. Therefore, God cannot punish Christ.
6. If God cannot punish Christ, penal substitution is false.

It follows that if God is perfectly just, then penal substitution is false.

One quick and easy way to deal with this objection would be to adopt
a consequentialist theory of justice. It is common coin that on consequentialist
theories of justice, punishment of the innocent may be justified, in view, for
example, of its deterrence value. In fact, one of the main criticisms of consequentialist theories of justice is precisely the fact that on such theories it may
be just to punish the innocent. A consequentialist penal theorist could fairly
easily provide justification for God's punishing Christ for our sins, namely, so
doing prevents the loss of the entire human race. So given a consequentialist
understanding of premise (1), we have no reason to think that premise (2) is
true.

But consequentialism seems ill-suited to serve as a basis for divine punishment because God's judgment is described in the Bible as ultimately eschato-
logical. The ungodly are "storing up wrath" for themselves for God's final day
of judgment (Rom 2.5). Punishment imposed at that point could seemingly
serve no other purpose than retribution. The Christian consequentialist could
say that punishment in hell does have a consequentialist justification, namely,
the sequestration of the wicked from the community of the redeemed, just as
hardened criminals are removed from society. But since God could achieve this
end by simply annihilating the damned, the consequentialist will need to find
some non-retributive reason for God's preserving them in existence. In any
case, the biblical view is that the wicked deserve punishment (Rom 1.32; Heb
10.29) and ascribes to God retribution (*ekdikēsis; avtapodoma*) for sins (Rom
11.9; 12.19), so that God's justice must be in some significant measure
retributive.

During the first half of the twentieth century, under the influence of social
scientists, retributive theories of justice were frowned upon in favor of consequentialist theories. Fortunately, there has been, over the last half-century or
so, a renaissance of theories of retributive justice, accompanied by a fading of

consequentialist theories,[24] so that we need not be distracted by the need to justify a retributive theory of justice. This change is due in no small part to the unwelcome implication of pure consequentialism that there are circumstances under which it is just to punish innocent people. Unfortunately, it is precisely the conviction that the innocent ought not to be punished that lies behind the claim that penal substitutionary atonement theories are unjust and immoral.

3.1.2.2   Responses to the Alleged Injustice of Penal Substitution

3.1.2.2.1 Penal Substitution without Punishment

It is not widely appreciated that this objection also has no purchase against penal substitution theorists who hold that God did not punish Christ for our sins, since they reject premise (6) in §3.1.2.1. Christ may be said to have voluntarily taken upon himself the suffering that would have been the punishment for our sins, had it been inflicted on us. He may even be said to have willingly paid the penalty for our sins. Our justice system permits people to pay penalties like fines on behalf of other persons without moral protest (Lewis 1997, p. 207). Since Christ was not punished for our sins, his voluntarily suffering on our behalf cannot be said to be unjust on God's part. So the objection is pressing only for penal substitution theorists who hold that God did punish Christ for our sins.

3.1.2.2.2 Metaethical Contextualization

Suppose that we do accept that God punished Christ. An assessment of premise (2) in §3.1.2.1 requires its contextualization within a metaethical theory about the grounding of objective moral values and duties. Who or what determines what is just/unjust? The proponents of penal substitution whom we have surveyed were, like Anselm, all proponents of some sort of Divine Command Theory of ethics, according to which moral duties are constituted by divine imperatives. There is no external law hanging over God to which He must conform. Since God does not issue commands to Himself, He literally has no moral duties to fulfill. He can act in any way consistent with His nature. He does not have the moral duties we have and will have unique prerogatives, such as giving and taking human life as He wills. He may usually act *in accordance with* duty, to borrow a Kantian phrase, but since He does not act *from* duty, He is

---

[24] See, e.g., White (2011); Tonry (2011). Ironically, some theologians, unaware of this sea change, denounce in the strongest terms a God of retributive justice (Finlan 2007, pp. 97–98), not realizing that their objection to the justice of penal substitution depends on a view of divine justice as retributive, lest God punish the innocent on consequentialist grounds. Moore (1989, ch. 5) gives a moving account of the horrendous results of consequentialism for our penal system.

free to make exceptions. This is the lesson of the astonishing story of God's commanding Abraham to sacrifice his son Isaac (Gen 22.1–19).

Now, if such a metaethical theory is even coherent, not to say true, as I have for wholly independent reasons argued it is (Moreland and Craig 2017, ch. 26, §5), then the present objection will have difficulty even getting off the ground.[25] As Grotius observed, even if God has established a system of justice among human beings that forbids the punishment of the innocent (and, hence, substitutionary punishment), He Himself is not so forbidden. He refused Moses's offer of himself as a substitutionary sacrifice, just as He refused the sacrificing of Isaac, but if He wills to take on human nature in the form of Jesus of Nazareth and give His own life as a sacrificial offering for sin, who is to forbid Him? He is free to do so as long as it is consistent with His nature. And what could be more consistent with our God's gracious nature than that He should condescend to take on our frail and fallen humanity and give His life to satisfy the demands of His own justice? The self-giving sacrifice of Christ exalts the nature of God by displaying His holy love.

3.1.2.2.3 The Nature of Retributive Justice

Perhaps the best face that can be put on the present objection is to claim that, contrary to Socinus, retributive justice is part of God's nature, and so it is impossible that He act contrary to the principles of retributive justice. Accordingly, premise (2) in §3.1.2.1 is true.

But that raises the question: what is retributive justice? The present objection does not sufficiently differentiate various accounts of retributivism. While a so-called *negative retributivism* holds that the innocent should not be punished because they do not deserve punishment, the essence of retributive justice lies in so-called *positive retributivism*, which holds that the guilty should be punished because they deserve punishment. What distinguishes retributivism as a theory of justice is the positive thesis that punishment of the guilty is an intrinsic good because the guilty deserve it. God is, as we have seen, a positive retributivist "who will by no means clear the guilty" (Exod 34.7). But the penal theorist may maintain that God is only qualifiedly a negative retributivist, since even if He has prohibited human beings from punishing innocent persons (Deut 24.16), and even if He is too good to Himself punish innocent human persons (Gen 18.25), still He reserves the prerogative to punish an innocent divine person, namely, Christ, in the place of the guilty. This extraordinary exception is a result of His goodness, not a defect in His justice. Hence, premise (2) in §3.1.2.1 is false.

---

[25] I have since discovered a forceful statement of this point by Plantinga (2011), pp. 113–14.

Lest positive retributivism be thought to be too thin a theory of retributive justice to ascribe to God, it should be noted how extraordinarily strong such a thesis is, so strong in fact that it has been criticized as utterly unrealistic on a human level. Zaibert indicts Michael Moore's claim that just desert constitutes a sufficient condition of punishment (i.e., the guilty should be punished because they deserve it) as entailing *legal moralism*, which would require the state to punish every moral wrong. Legal moralism would require "an impossibly large criminal justice apparatus" that would be "utterly unmanageable and unrealistic" (Zaibert 2006, p. 161). Even outside the context of the state, the implausibility of punishing every immorality is so high that even the staunchest unbridled retributivist has to admit that such a suggestion must be rejected. It is arguably impossible to do this, Zaibert exclaims, without going crazy (2006, pp. 183–85). The theist can only smile at this secular theorist's huffing and puffing about a task for which God alone is qualified and capable of carrying out. But at least we see therein how robust is a positive retributive theory of justice, which can then be further augmented by taking God to be a qualified negative retributivist as well.

This response suffices to dispense with the objection; but even more can be said.

3.1.2.2.4 Prima Facie vs. Ultima Facie Justification of Punishment

The objection based on premise (2) in §3.1.2.1 also fails to reckon with the fact that the prima facie demands of retributive justice can be outweighed in specific cases by weightier moral considerations, so that punishment in such a case may (or may not) be justified ultima facie. Theorists often make this point by distinguishing between justification of the *practice* of punishment and justification of an *act* of punishment. When positive retributivists claim that the guilty should be punished, they are talking about justification of the general practice of punishment, not about specific cases. In specific cases, the act of punishment may not be required in light of overriding considerations, for example, protecting the rights of others or securing a plea bargain in order that persons guilty of even more heinous crimes can be punished (Morison 2005, pp. 77–86). In such a case the demands of retributive justice are waived.

So, Feinberg and Gross observe that there are occasions on which a person can be fully justified in voluntarily producing an unjust effect upon another person. Person *A* may be justified in violating person *B*'s rights when there is no third alternative open to him; but that justification does not cancel the injustice done to *B*. Drawing upon Aristotle's distinction between the just/unjust *quality* of an act and the just/unjust *effect* of an act upon others, they state:

> In that case, we can say that *B* was unjustly *treated* although *A*'s act
> resulting in that effect was not an instance of unjust *behavior*. For an act
> to have an unjust quality (whatever its effects) it must be, objectively
> speaking, the wrong thing to do in the circumstances, unexcused and
> unjustified, voluntarily undertaken, and deliberately chosen by an unrushed
> actor who is well aware of the alternatives open to him. (Feinberg and Gross
> 1980, p. 286)

Similarly, even if God's essential justice includes unqualified negative
retributivism, the prima facie demands of negative retributive justice may be
overridden in the case of Christ. In the case of the death of Christ, the penal
theorist might claim that God is fully justified in waiving the demands of
negative retributive justice for the sake of the salvation of mankind. Biblical
scholar Donald Carson reminds us:

> It is the *unjust* punishment of the Servant in Isaiah 53 that is so remarkable.
> Forgiveness, restoration, salvation, reconciliation – all are possible, not
> because sins have somehow been canceled as if they never were, but because
> another bore them *unjustly*. But by this adverb 'unjustly' I mean that the
> person who bore them was just and did not deserve the punishment, not that
> some moral 'system' that God was administering was thereby distorted.
> (Carson 2004, p. 133)

The penal substitution theorist might maintain that in the specific case of
Christ's death, the demands of negative retributive justice were overridden by
weightier moral considerations.

Even the staunchest of contemporary retributivists, Michael Moore, recognizes that the demands of retributive justice are prima facie demands that can be
and are overridden in specific cases. That is why Moore is not committed, as
Zaibert imagines, to legal moralism. Moore says that we must not confuse the
intrinsic goodness of retribution with the categorical duty to carry out retributive justice on every possible occasion. He calls himself a "threshold deontologist," that is to say, he abides by the categorical norm of morality until doing
so produces sufficiently bad consequences as to pass some threshold (Moore
1997, p. 158). So in the extreme case where one must punish an innocent person
or else the world will be totally destroyed, one should punish the person.
The penal substitution theorist could similarly claim that God, by waiving the
prima facie demands of negative retributive justice and punishing Christ for our
sins, has mercifully saved the world from total destruction and was therefore
acting compatibly with moral goodness.

Now it might be asked why, if there are weightier considerations prompting
God to waive the demands of negative retributive justice in Christ's case, He
did not instead waive the demands of positive retributive justice and offer

everyone a general pardon for sin. As we have seen, many of the Church Fathers freely embraced this possibility, as did Aquinas and Grotius after them. But these thinkers also held that God had good reasons for achieving atonement through Christ's passion. As Abelard and Grotius saw, so doing was a powerful display of both God's love of people and His hatred of sin, which has proved powerfully attractive throughout history in drawing people to faith in Christ, especially as they themselves face innocent suffering. God's pardoning sin without satisfaction does not, despite first appearances, imply universalism, for God's pardon may still require its free acceptance by people. It is not at all implausible that a world in which there occurs the great demonstration of God's love and holiness in the vicarious suffering and death of Christ is a world in which a more optimal number of people come freely to embrace salvation than a world in which free pardon without cost or consequence is offered men. The counterfactuals involved are too speculative to permit us to claim that a general pardon would have been more effective in accomplishing God's ends. Besides, substitutionary punishment of Christ permits God to relax far less His essential retributive justice for the sake of mercy than would be the case with a general pardon, thereby expressing more fully His essential character of holy love.

3.1.2.2.5 Punishment and the Imputation of Sins

But suppose that the prima facie demands of negative retributive justice are essential to God and could not be overridden, so that premise (2) in §3.1.2.1 is true. Would God be unjust to punish Christ? Not necessarily. For consider premise (4) in §3.1.2.1. Up to this point we have acquiesced in the assumption that Christ was, indeed, innocent. But for penal theorists like Turretin, who affirm the imputation of our sins to Christ, there is no question in Christ's case of God's punishing the innocent and so violating even the prima facie demands of negative retributive justice. For Christ, in virtue of the imputation of our sins to him, was legally guilty before God. Of course, because our sins were merely imputed to Christ and not infused in him, Christ was, as always, personally virtuous, a paradigm of compassion, selflessness, purity, and courage, but he was declared legally guilty before God. Therefore, he was legally liable to punishment. Thus, given the doctrine of the imputation of sins, the present objection to penal substitutionary theories is a non-starter, being based on the false assumption of premise (4).

We saw in §3.1.1.2.4 that imputation of wrongdoing or guilt to a blameless party is a coherent and widely accepted feature of our justice system. Now sometimes the ascription of vicarious liability is denounced as unjust, though tolerated as a sort of necessary evil due to practical considerations arising from the human impossibility of administering a system of pure justice. That only serves to reinforce the point made previously, that the prima facie demands of retributive justice can be outweighed by greater goods. But when would the imposition of vicarious liability be even prima facie unjust? Arguably, it could be only in cases in which it is nonvoluntary. If an employer, out of personal concern for his employee, wishes to act mercifully by voluntarily being held vicariously liable for his employee's wrongdoing, how is that unjust or immoral? In the same way, if Christ voluntarily invites our sins to be imputed to him for the sake of our salvation, what injustice is there in this? Who is to gainsay him?

In sum, the objection to penal substitution based on the justification of punishment is insufficiently nuanced. It applies only to theories that affirm that Christ was punished for our sins. It makes unwarranted assumptions about the ontological foundations of moral duty independent of God's commands. It presupposes without warrant that God is by nature an unqualified negative retributivist. It overlooks the possibility that the prima facie demands of negative retributive justice might be overridden in Christ's case. And it takes for granted that Christ was legally innocent, in opposition to the doctrine of imputation. It thus fails to show any injustice in God's punishing Christ in our place.

3.2 Satisfaction of Divine Justice

A biblically adequate atonement theory must not only include penal substitution as a central facet; it must also include propitiation, the appeasement of God's just wrath against sin. The source of God's wrath is His retributive justice, and so appeasement of wrath is a matter of the satisfaction of divine justice. We have seen that biblically the satisfaction of God's justice primarily takes place, not as Anselm thought, through compensation, but through substitutionary punishment.[26]

Here the superiority of a theory involving Christ's punishment emerges over penal theories according to which God does not punish Christ. For it is hard to see how divine justice could be satisfied by Christ's voluntarily taking suffering upon himself if it were not a punishment meted out for our sins. If the punishment for an offense were, say, deportation, how could justice be satisfied by someone else's voluntarily going or being sent into

---

[26] However, Murphy's suggestion is worth exploring, that just as an offense can demand not only punishment under criminal law but also compensatory damages under civil law, so our sins might demand not only Christ's being punished but also his giving compensation to God (Murphy 2009, pp. 272–73).

exile unless it were intended to be a punishment for the wrongdoing in question? If the suffering or harsh treatment is not punishment, then the demands of retributive justice seem to go unsatisfied.

3.2.1 The Alleged Unsatisfactoriness of Penal Substitution

It might be objected that neither could penal substitution possibly meet the demands of divine retributive justice. For punishing another person for my crimes would not serve to remove my liability to punishment. So how can penal substitution satisfy God's justice? We can formulate this objection as follows:

1. Unless the person who committed a wrong is punished for that wrong, divine justice is not satisfied.
2. If God practices penal substitution, then the person who committed a wrong is not punished for that wrong.
3. Therefore, if God practices penal substitution, divine justice is not satisfied.

3.2.2 Responses to the Alleged Unsatisfactoriness of Penal Substitution

3.2.2.1 Metaethical Contextualization

Let us consider premise (1) of §3.2.1. Once the question of the satisfaction of divine justice is contextualized, as it must be, within a broader metaethical theory like Divine Command Theory, then the objection becomes rather odd. For on Judaeo-Christian theism God is the Legislator, Judge, and Ruler of the moral realm. Contrast the U.S. separation of powers, according to which Congress defines crimes and their punishments, the judiciary interprets and applies those laws and punishments, and the executive holds the power of pardon (Crouch 2009, p. 14). In God's case all these powers are vested in the same individual. So if He determines that the demands of justice are met by Christ's punishment, who is to gainsay Him? He is the source of the moral law, its interpreter, and its executor. He Himself determines what meets justice's demands. So what is the problem?

This response might seem to imply an account of satisfaction as so-called *acceptation*. The medieval theologian John Duns Scotus suggested that God might have accepted any sacrifice He pleased as satisfactory for the demands of His retributive justice. Defenders of penal substitution have not been sympathetic to acceptation accounts (e.g., Crisp 2011). For then God might have accepted as satisfactory the death of any ordinary human being or even an animal. But then it is not true, as Scripture affirms, that "it is impossible that the blood of bulls and goats should take away sins" (Heb 10.4). Retributive theories of justice require that the punishment be proportionate to the crime if justice is to be satisfied. The objector to substitutionary satisfaction would find a sympathetic ear among penal substitution theorists, if he affirmed that retributive justice, as we know and understand it, is essential to God's nature and so could not be satisfied by mere animal sacrifices. But then how does the punishment of Christ satisfy the demands of retributive justice?

3.2.2.2 Imputation and Satisfaction of Justice

David Lewis argues that our justice system remains deeply conflicted about whether a substitute can satisfy the demands of justice. He claims that criminal law does permit substitutionary punishment in some cases. A friend can pay a person's fine if both agree to the arrangement. "Yet this is just as much a case of penal substitution as the others" (Lewis 1997, p. 207). Lewis rejects the view espoused by expressivists that these penalties are not really punishments. Some of these fines, Lewis remarks, are just as burdensome as prison sentences – and, we might add, just as censorious. If we were single-mindedly against penal substitution, Lewis says, then we should conclude that fines are an *unsatisfactory* form of punishment, that such punishment, in other words, fails to satisfy justice's demands. But we do not.[27] Lewis draws the lesson that penal substitution may sometimes satisfy justice's demands, just as the Reformers maintained.

Moreover, criminal law also seems to involve further instances of penal substitution. In criminal cases involving vicarious liability, the guilt of a subordinate for his actions may be imputed to an innocent superior. Both parties are held guilty for the wrongdoing, and either (or both) may be punished. But if the superior, for example, chooses to bear the full weight of punishment, then the subordinate will not and may not be punished for those crimes. The superior is punished for those crimes, which satisfies justice both for him and for his subordinate. This looks for all the world like penal substitution.

The lesson we have learned from cases of vicarious liability is that the demands of retributive justice are frequently met by persons other than the person who committed the wrong. What is required for the satisfaction of justice is at most that only persons who are liable for a wrong are punished for that wrong. Accordingly, premise (1) in §3.2.1 should be revised to

---

[27] In response to Lewis, Quinn makes the interesting observation that courts have sometimes expressed diffidence about allowing companies to purchase insurance policies to cover possible penalties (Quinn 2004, pp. 722–30). But such cases do not show that penal substitution is unsatisfactory; rather, they furnish a good example of the way in which ultima facie considerations can justify penal substitution, thereby meeting justice's demands in a specific action.

1*. Unless a person who is liable for a wrong is punished for that wrong, divine justice is not satisfied.

But then given the doctrine of the imputation of sin, Christ is legally liable for our sins and so may satisfy divine justice by being duly punished for those sins.

3.2.2.3 Punishment of a Divinely Appointed Substitute and Representative

3.2.2.3.1 Substitution and Representation

The previous considerations suffice to dispense with the objection. But now consider premise (2) in §3.2.1 as well. In cases of penal substitution is it always the case that the person who did the wrong is not punished for that wrong? Contemporary theologians have disputed the point by distinguishing between exclusionary place taking (*exkludierende Stellvertretung*) and inclusionary place taking (*inkludierende Stellvertretung*). This important distinction requires a word of explanation about substitution and representation, respectively. In cases of simple substitution, someone takes the place of another person but does not represent that person. For example, a pinch hitter in baseball enters the lineup to bat in the place of another player. He is a substitute for that player but in no sense represents that other player. That is why the batting average of the player whom he replaces is not affected by the pinch hitter's performance. On the other hand, a simple representative acts on behalf of another person and serves as his spokesman but is not a substitute for that person. For example, the baseball player has an agent who represents him in contract negotiations with the team. The representative does not replace the player but merely advocates for him.[28]

These roles can be combined, in which case we have neither simple substitution nor simple representation but rather substitutional representation (or representative substitution). A good illustration of this combination of substitution and representation is to be found in the role of a proxy at a shareholders' meeting. If we cannot attend the meeting ourselves, we may sign an agreement authorizing someone else to serve as our proxy at the meeting. He votes for us, and because he has been authorized to do so, his votes are our votes: we have voted via proxy at the meeting of shareholders. The proxy is a substitute in that he attends the meeting in our place, but he is also our representative in that he

---

[28] Representation in this sense needs to be distinguished from representation in the sense of symbolization. A baseball scorecard is a representation of the playing field, and marks on it represent hits, outs, runs, and so on. Christ's death as a representation in this sense would be akin to the popular misunderstanding of the governmental theory as a representation to the world of what it would look like if Christ were punished for our sins.

does not vote instead of us but on our behalf, so that we vote. This combination is an inclusionary place taking.

3.2.2.3.2 Christ as Our Substitute and Representative

As we have seen, Turretin believes that Christ, in bearing our punishment, was both our substitute and our representative before God. He was punished in our place and bore the suffering we deserved. But he also represented us before God, so that his punishment was our punishment. Christ was not merely punished instead of us, rather, we were punished by proxy. For that reason, divine justice is satisfied.[29]

How is it that we are so represented by Christ? Turretin, it will be recalled, proposed two ways in which we are in union with Christ; first, by way of his incarnation, and second, by way of our mystical union with him. Although theologians often appeal to this latter union of believers with Christ to explain the efficacy of his atonement, such an account seems to be viciously circular. In Turretin's view, it is union with Christ that is the basis of the imputation of sins and our justification. But the problem is that the mystical union of believers with Christ is the privilege only of persons who are regenerate and justified. There is here a vicious explanatory circle: in order to be in mystical union with Christ one must first be justified, but in order to be justified one must first be in mystical union with Christ. What is needed is a union with Christ that is explanatorily prior to (even if chronologically simultaneous with) imputation and justification.

Turretin's first proposal is therefore to be preferred.[30] In virtue of Christ's incarnation (and, I should say, his baptism, whereby Jesus identified himself with fallen humanity), Christ is appointed by God to serve as our proxy before Him. The Logos, the second person of the Trinity, has voluntarily consented to serve as our proxy before God by means of his incarnation and baptism, so that by his death he might satisfy the demands of divine justice on our behalf.

3.2.2.4   Socinus's Objections

As for Socinus's several arguments against Christ's death being sufficient to satisfy for humanity's sins, I consider Turretin's responses based upon the deity

---

[29] Atonement theorists have identified examples of such punishment by proxy even in human affairs, such as a team captain's being punished for his team's failings or a squad leader's being punished for his troops' failings (Porter 2004, pp. 236–37). Of course, Christ has been uniquely appointed by God to be our proxy, which may make his case *sui generis*.

[30] So-called realist accounts of the union, according to which humanity is one metaphysical entity (Crisp 2009, pp. 437–46), are utterly implausible and unavailing, being dependent upon a tenseless theory of time and implying a view of human personhood incompatible with divine punishment and rewards (Craig 2001, ch. 5).

of Christ to be entirely adequate. Turretin's analysis of Christ's punishment as God the Father's withdrawing from him the beatific vision and suspending the joy, comfort, sense, and fruition of full felicity comports well with the model of the incarnation I have elsewhere proposed, whereby the Logos in his waking, human consciousness is bereaved of these blessings (Moreland and Craig 2017, pp. 607–09). It is the divine Logos himself who suffers these bereavements in his human nature. Moreover, because of the divinity of his person, the suffering of God the Son, who had never experienced anything other than intimacy with the Father, has an infinite value, more than sufficient to pay the penalty due for every sin that ever has been or will be committed.

Herein we see the organic connection between Christ's atoning death and resurrection. God's raising Jesus from the dead is not only a ratification to us of the efficacy of Christ's atoning death; it is a necessary consequence of it. For by his substitutionary death Christ fully satisfied divine justice. The penalty of death having been fully paid, Christ can no more remain dead than a criminal who has fully served his sentence can remain imprisoned. Punishment cannot justly continue; justice demands his release. Thus, Christ's resurrection is both a necessary consequence and a ratification of his satisfaction of divine justice.

3.3 Redemption

Redemption through Christ's blood will be a third, vital part of any biblical atonement theory. Christ's atoning death frees us from the bondage of sin, death, and hell and so liberates us from Satan's power. In Wesley's words:

> He breaks the power of canceled sin,
> He sets the prisoner free,
> His blood can make the foulest clean,
> His blood availed for me.
> ("O For a Thousand Tongues to Sing" 1740)

Contemporary *Christus Victor* or redemption theorists recognize that the ransom price of our redemption need not be thought of as paid to Satan to secure our release from bondage. Rather, the ransom price is paid to God to discharge the debt of punishment we owe to divine justice. Just as we speak of a criminal's having "paid his debt to society" by suffering the punishment for his crime, so we may speak of Christ's having paid the debt we owe to God. Talk of ransom is thus a metaphor for penal substitution. Atonement theories emphasizing redemption are thus not stand-alone theories but are a facet of an atonement theory that has penal substitution at the center.

3.3.1 Divine Forgiveness as Legal Pardon

How are condemned prisoners set free? If they are not to endure further punishment, they must receive a full pardon. I mentioned earlier that the biblical material on divine forgiveness suggests that it is more accurate to think of divine forgiveness on the analogy of a legal pardon by a Ruler rather than on the analogy of the forgiveness extended by a private person. For as we have seen, God's forgiveness accomplishes much more than a change of attitude toward sinners on God's part. God's forgiving sins removes our liability to punishment and thus obviates the demands of retributive justice upon us: the just desert of our sins is gone. It is evident, then, that divine forgiveness is much more akin to legal pardon than to forgiveness as typically understood. Kathleen Moore has made the point forcefully by observing that when people ask God to forgive their sins, they are clearly hoping that God will not inflict the full measure of punishment they know they deserve. "These people would discover the seriousness of their conceptual confusion if God forgave their sins and punished them nevertheless – which is always an option for God" (Moore 1989, p. 184).

3.3.2 Pardon and Its Effects

It therefore behooves us to look more closely at the nature of legal pardon and its effects.

3.3.2.1 Pardon

What is a pardon? Chief Justice John Marshall, in a landmark decision, describes a pardon as follows:

> A pardon is an act of grace, proceeding from the power entrusted with the execution of the laws, which exempts the individual, on whom it is bestowed, from the punishment the law inflicts for a crime he has committed. (*United States v. Wilson*, 32 U.S. 150 [1833])

According to Marshall's characterization, a pardon is an act of mercy, coming from the person(s) possessing the power of the executive, which removes a criminal's liability to punishment for a specific crime he has committed. Marshall's description seems an apt characterization of a divine pardon as well. God is the power Who executes His divine torah, and His pardon is an act of grace by which He exempts elect sinners, who have violated His law, from the punishment they deserve. Every element of Marshall's definition finds a theological analogue. No wonder Daniel Kobil characterizes Marshall's vision of a pardon as "something akin to divine forgiveness" (Kobil 1991, p. 594)!

3.3.2.2 Effects of a Pardon

What are the effects of a pardon? Marshall says that it exempts the individual from the punishment prescribed by the law for his crime. This much is uncontroversial. The controversial question is whether a pardon serves to expunge the criminal's guilt.

3.3.2.2.1 Opinion in Garland

Following English precedent, the U.S. courts were at first emphatic as to the effect of a pardon in expiating guilt. In *Ex parte Garland* (1866) the Supreme Court famously declared:

> The inquiry arises as to the effect and operation of a pardon, and on this point all the authorities concur. A pardon reaches both the punishment prescribed for the offence and the guilt of the offender; and when the pardon is full, it releases the punishment and blots out of existence the guilt, so that in the eye of the law the offender is as innocent as if he had never committed the offence. If granted before conviction, it prevents any of the penalties and disabilities consequent upon conviction from attaching; if granted after conviction, it removes the penalties and disabilities, and restores him to all his civil rights; it makes him, as it were, a new man, and gives him a new credit and capacity. (*Ex parte Garland*, 71 U.S. 333, 380–81 [1866])

Like Marshall's description of a pardon, this characterization of the effects of a full pardon is a marvelous description of a divine pardon. "If anyone is in Christ, he is a new creation; the old has passed away, behold, the new has come" (II Cor 5.17). The pardoned sinner's guilt is expiated, so that he is legally innocent before God.

3.3.2.2.2 Garland Challenged

But as a description of the effects of human pardons, *Garland*'s sweeping assertions have been eroded by subsequent court decisions.[31] In the *Harvard Law Review* of 1915 Samuel Williston published an influential article, "Does a Pardon Blot Out Guilt?", in which he criticized *Garland* and its judicial progeny, and which has been frequently cited by the courts. Williston complained, "Everybody ... knows that the vast majority of pardoned convicts were in fact guilty; and when it is said that in the eye of the law they are as innocent as if they have never committed an offense, the natural rejoinder is, then the eyesight of the law is very bad" (Williston 1915, p. 648). The truth,

---

[31] For a thorough review of the relevant judicial decisions, see *In re Sang Man Shin*, 125 Nev. 100, 104–09 (2009); *Robertson v. Shinseki*, 26 Vet. App. 169, 176–79 (2013).

says Williston, is rather as Lord Coke wrote: *Poena mori potest, culpa perennis erit.*[32] A moment's reflection suggests that Williston must understand by "guilt" simply the property or fact of having committed the crime. On this understanding, to be guilty of a crime is just to have committed the crime.

According to Williston:

> The true line of distinction seems to be this: The pardon removes all legal punishment for the offense. Therefore if the mere conviction involves certain disqualifications which would not follow from the commission of the crime without conviction, the pardon removes such disqualifications. On the other hand, if character is a necessary qualification and the commission of the crime would disqualify even though there had been no criminal prosecution for the crime, the fact that the criminal has been convicted and pardoned does not make him anymore eligible. (Williston 1915, p. 653)

The point is this: a pardon removes the legal consequences (such as abridgement of civil rights) resulting from the fact of conviction, but a pardon does not affect any disqualifications resulting from the commission of the crime. The fact that a crime has been committed cannot be erased. It is this fact that Williston identifies as guilt. Though pardoned, the person still stole or lied or acted recklessly and so remains guilty of the crime he committed. As such he may, despite his pardon, be disqualified from certain activities, such as giving testimony or practicing law. Henry Weihofen, in a later review, citing Williston, concludes that the effect of a pardon (other than on grounds of innocence) is "to absolve from further punishment and restore civil rights, but *not to undo what is past or blot out of existence a fact*, namely, that *the person has committed a crime and been sentenced and punished* for it" (Weihofen 1939, p. 181, my emphasis).

An examination of various district, state, and appellate court cases walking back the assertions of *Garland* reveals that the courts in such cases tend to presuppose this same understanding of guilt as the property of having committed a crime.[33] These cases have typically to do with whether a pardon serves to expunge one's criminal record or to remove a particular disqualification (such as disbarment, banishment from the trading floor, or denial of veteran's benefits) suffered by the pardonee as a consequence of his being convicted of

---

[32] "Punishment may expire, but guilt will last forever."

[33] See, e.g., *Groseclose v. Plummer* 106 F.2d 311, 313 (9th Cir.1939); *People ex rel. Prisament v. Brophy* 287 N.Y. 132, 137–38 (1941); *State Ex Rel. Wier v. Peterson*, 369 A.2d.1076, 1080, 1081 (Del.1976); *Dixon v. McMullen* 527 F. Supp. 711, 717–18 (N.D.Tex.1981); *In re Abrams*, 689 A.2d 6, 7, 10–11 (D.C. 1997); *R.J.L. v. State,* 887 So.2d 1268, 1280–81(Fla.2004); *Hirschberg v. Commodity Futures Trading Com'n*, 414 F.3d 679, 682, 683 (2005); *Fletcher v. Graham,* 192 S.W.3d 350, 362–63 (Ky.2006); *In re Sang Man Shin*, 125 Nev. 100, 110 (2009); *Robertson v. Shinseki*, 26 Vet. App. 169, 179 (2013).

the crime for which he received a pardon. In holding that *Garland* overstepped in asserting that a pardon blots out guilt because a pardon does not blot out the past conduct leading to the conviction, these courts equate guilt with having carried out the conduct that led to the conviction.[34]

3.3.2.2.3 Garland *Exonerated*

While such an understanding of the word "guilt" may accord with much of ordinary language, a little reflection reveals that, given standard retributive theories of justice, such a conception of guilt has bizarre consequences. For on this view a person's guilt could never be expunged, whether by pardon or punishment.[35]

Even if a person has served his full sentence and so satisfied the demands of justice, he remains guilty, since it will be ineradicably and forever the case that once upon a time he did commit the crime. But then on standard theories of retributive justice, he still deserves punishment! For it is an axiom of retributive justice that the guilty deserve punishment. Such an understanding of guilt would thus, in effect, sentence everyone to hell, even for the most minor of crimes, since guilt could never be eradicated and, hence, the demands of justice satisfied. Indeed, even a divine pardon would not serve to remove guilt and save us from punishment, since even God cannot change the past. But such a conclusion is incoherent, since it is the function of pardon to cancel one's liability to punishment. Therefore, this understanding of guilt is incompatible with standard theories of retributive justice.

The *Garland* court and its progeny should not be thought to consider a pardon to be a sort of judicial time machine, capable of erasing the past. It is logically incoherent to bring it about that an event that has occurred has not occurred, and it would be ungracious to attribute to our courts the absurd

---

[34] So also Steiner (1997), who, without ever defining "guilt," claims that it is "illogical to assert that the pardon 'blots out of existence the guilt' of the offender," since "the acts leading to the conviction, whether or not they are punished, remain." She observes that after Williston's article, courts generally adopted one of three views regarding the effects of a presidential pardon: (i) a pardon obliterates both the conviction and the guilt; (ii) a pardon obliterates the conviction but not the guilt; or (iii) a pardon obliterates neither the conviction nor the guilt. She takes no cognizance of a fourth alternative staring us in the face, namely, (iv) a pardon obliterates the guilt but not the conviction. Alternatives (ii) and (iii) are incoherent, as explained in the text, since guilt could never be expunged. Although some courts seemingly affirmed (i), *Garland* does not affirm that a pardon blots out the offense or the conviction. Accordingly, *Garland* and its progeny are best interpreted as affirming (iv).

[35] In criminal law, guilt is typically determined by a wrongful act (*actus reus*) and a blameworthy mental state (*mens rea*). Obviously, neither punishment nor pardon annuls the fact that a person committed a certain act in the past nor the fact that that act was wrong. Nor does it annul the fact that the person acted intentionally and without excuse. But these are the conditions Moore identifies as just desert (1997, pp. 33, 91, 168, 403–04).

opinion that a pardon can erase from the past a person's wrongdoing or conviction for a crime. Rather, what the *Garland* court was doing, and what its detractors have failed to do, is what contemporary philosophers of time call "taking tense seriously".[36] When the Supreme Court declared that a pardon "blots out of existence the guilt, so that in the eye of the law the offender is as innocent as if he had never committed the offence," it takes seriously the tenses of the verbs involved. It recognizes that the offender *was* guilty, but as a result of his pardon he *is now* innocent in the law's eyes. Moreover, the counterfactual conditional signaled by "as if" reveals that the law is not blind to his offense. The law can see his offense, but as a result of the pardon the offender is now as innocent as he would have been if he had never committed the offense.

Moreover, contrary to the opinions of some lower courts,[37] *Garland* is wholly consistent with the Supreme Court's opinion in *Burdick v. United States*, 236 U.S. 79 (1915) that the pardon of an accused person, if accepted, actually implies his guilt (otherwise there would be nothing to be pardoned). *Garland* has no interest in denying that the offender *was* guilty, so that the pardon, in taking away his guilt, implies that he was guilty. A pardon does not have an appellate function, as the courts have recognized, in that it does not imply a miscarriage of justice; the correctness of the guilty verdict rendered is not undermined. But now the person is pardoned, and so the effect of that verdict is canceled: though once guilty, the pardonee no longer is.[38]

The opinion in *Garland* is thus fully in accord with the prevailing view that a pardon has no effect upon the criminal conduct and conviction of the person pardoned. *Garland* is thus in accord with the prevailing opinion that a pardon serves to release a person from all the legal consequences of his conviction, including punishment, taken in abstraction from the wrongdoing itself.

It is obvious that the *Garland* court has a very different conception of guilt than lower courts that see themselves as departing from *Garland*. Rather than equate guilt with the facticity of a past event, *Garland* assumes that guilt is a property that can be temporarily exemplified and then lost though pardon or appropriate

---

[36] The phrase was apparently inspired by the great Oxford tense logician A. N. Prior, who, in reaction to W. V. O. Quine's extolling the tenselessness of modern logic, praised medieval logic because it "took tenses far more seriously than our own common logic does" (Prior 1958, 117). I'm grateful to Prior scholar David Jakobsen for alerting me to Prior's article, which was originally Prior's presidential address to the New Zealand Congress of Philosophy in 1954.

[37] E.g., *In re Sang Man Shin*, 125 Nev. 100, 105 (2009).

[38] A number of scholars have noted that pardons differ from other forms of executive clemency in that the latter, unlike pardons, leave intact the judgment of guilt. For example, President Carter, in proclaiming an amnesty for Vietnam War draft-dodgers, said poignantly that their crimes have been forgotten, not forgiven. Similarly, recipients of commutations and reprieves remain guilty (Kobil 1991, p. 577; Caplow 2013, p. 299; Messing 2016, p. 672; Schoenburg 2016, p. 924). This distinction seems to make sense only if a pardon annuls the guilt of the offender.

punishment. So what is this property? It seems to me that the most perspicuous understanding of guilt in this sense is that it is *liability to punishment*. Guilty verdicts in cases of strict liability (in which there may be neither wrongdoing nor culpability) show that guilt cannot be equated merely with culpable wrongdoing. Rather, a verdict of "Guilty" is plausibly a declaration that the person is legally liable to punishment. To be guilty of a crime is to be legally liable to punishment for that crime. Such an understanding of guilt makes it perspicuous why punishment or pardon serves to expiate guilt. A person who has served his sentence has paid his debt to society, and so is now no longer guilty; that is to say, no longer liable to punishment. Similarly, a person who has been pardoned is by all accounts no longer liable to punishment for the crime he committed.

To return, then, to the concerns of theology, it seems to me that *Garland's* statement of the effects of a pardon is a wonderful description of the effects of a divine pardon of a person's sins. By taking tense seriously, we understand how a person who was once guilty may, in virtue of a divine pardon, be no longer guilty, despite the ineradicable fact that he did commit the sin for which he was justly condemned. Like punishment, a pardon expiates a person's legal guilt so that he is no longer condemned and liable to punishment.

3.3.3 Pardon, Mercy, and Justice

3.3.3.1 Pardon as an Act of Grace

The question arises as to the grounds on which God can pardon our sins. This brings us to the controversial question whether pardons are acts of mercy, and if so, what justifies such an act of clemency. H. R. T. Roberts provides a rough working explication of acting mercifully: "In all justice I am entitled to A from *x*, but it is *mine* to exact and I choose not to" (Roberts 1971, p. 353). Alwynne Smart would add that the choice is made "solely through benevolence," and not, for example, out of constraint, self-interest, or ulterior motives (Smart 1968, p. 359). Samuel Morison makes the application to executive pardons:

> The institutional expression of mercy through executive clemency means . . . the partial or complete mitigation of justly imposed punishment (including the removal of the collateral consequences attendant upon a felony conviction) by the chief executive on *non-retributive* grounds, that is to say, for reasons which do not necessarily have anything to do with what a criminal justly deserves as punishment for the commission of a particular offense. (Morison 2005, pp. 18–19)

The central question to be answered here, in Moore's words, is this: given a retributivist theory of justice and of the role of the state, under what conditions is a pardon justified and under what conditions is it not justified? (Moore 1989, p. 9).

3.3.3.2   Challenge of Pure Retributivism

As we have seen, early Supreme Court opinions considered pardons to be acts of grace on the part of the executive power. Pure retributivists like Kathleen Moore have, however, sharply challenged the validity of pardons issued solely on grounds of mercy.[39] These theorists argue that pardons given for any other reason than furthering justice are of necessity unjust and therefore immoral. In particular, pardons given out of mercy violate the principles of (positive) retributive justice because in such cases the guilty do not receive their just desert. To pardon someone out of mercy is therefore to subvert justice and to act unjustly.

The claim of the pure retributivists has enormous theological implications for divine pardon. For God is portrayed in the Bible as acting mercifully toward us and His pardoning our sins as an act of grace (Eph 2.8–9; Rom 9.16). At the same time, the Bible portrays God as a positive retributivist with respect to justice. Indeed, it is plausible, I think, that retributive justice belongs essentially to God. Brian Leftow observes that "the more central and prominent an attribute is in the Biblical picture of God, the stronger the case for taking it to be necessary to being God, *ceteris paribus*: this is the only reason philosophers usually treat being omniscient or omnipotent as thus necessary" (Leftow 2012, p. 412). It is hard to think of an attribute more central and prominent in the biblical picture of God than His righteousness or justice (Owen [n.d.]). It would have been inconceivable to the biblical authors that God might act unjustly (Rom 9.14).

But now God faces a dilemma: if a pardon is given to rectify some injustice, then the pardon is not an act of grace given out of mercy but is an expression of justice; if it is given out of mercy, then the executive violates the principles of retributive justice and is unjust. Clearly, God cannot give pardons to rectify some injustice, since His judicial condemnation of sinners is perfectly just. If He pardons, it must be out of mercy. But then He would seem to be acting unjustly. But given that retributive justice belongs to God's character, it is impossible that He so act. He must give people what they deserve, on pain of acting contrary to His own nature.

3.3.3.3   Response to the Retributivist Challenge

Critics of the pure retributivists have argued that the prima facie demands of retributive justice can be overridden by other considerations, so that the

---

[39] For literature, see Morison (2005, p. 4).

executive who pardons out of sheer mercy is not immoral. In a recent, lengthy review of the question, Samuel Morison argues that sometimes leniency is morally justified when satisfying the prima facie demands of retributive justice is immoral or practically impossible. What is striking about Morison's concerns is that none of them, such as protecting people against self-incrimination, unreasonable searches and seizures, and so on, is remotely relevant to the case of God's administration of justice. In fact, it is telling when Morison quotes approvingly Murphy's declamation, "The liberal tradition would thus view it as silly (and perhaps impious) to make God's ultimate justice the model for the state's legal justice; and thus any attempt to identify *criminal* with *sinner* is to be avoided" (Murphy 1985, cited by Morison 2005, p. 84). In fact, Morison states plainly, "The pursuit of the legitimate interest in securing social peace via state-sponsored legal punishment (as distinguished from divine retribution) does not entail any prima facie obligation to exact the full measure of morally justified punitive suffering merely because the offender deserves it" (Morison 2005, p. 86). Morison thus recognizes God's obligation to exact the full measure of morally justified punitive suffering.

Morison's defense of pardons on grounds of mercy is the fullest I have encountered in the literature, and yet it is stunningly irrelevant, as he recognizes, to the case of divine pardon. In the end Morison rejects "the implicit conflation of morality and justice, which assumes that the legitimate exercise of mercy always must be consistent with the demands of justice" (Morison 2005, p. 100). He cites George Rainbolt: "The fact that mercy counsels unjust acts on occasion does not imply that it is a vice. It only reflects the unfortunate fact that mercy and justice can conflict" (cited by Morison 2005, p. 101). But that is precisely the problem for the Christian theist: God's justice and mercy are both essential to Him and so neither can be sacrificed. We can agree with Morison "that the moral basis for the merciful extension of clemency is thus whatever 'is right and good as judged against *all* moral considerations, rather than only those of justice. *Any* pertinent moral consideration may be taken into account'" (Morison 2005, p. 104, citing Brien 1998, p. 91, with emphasis added). One should not, indeed, simply identify morality with justice. But none of the considerations that Morison has adduced for tempering justice with mercy in the case of the state applies to God. So how can God legitimately exercise mercy if doing so is inconsistent with the demands of His justice? Morison admits that "there is no tidy conceptual solution to the problem of reconciling justice and mercy in the abstract" (Morison 2005, p. 102). He concludes that "the practice of punishment is informed by a plurality of values that may not be ultimately commensurable" (Morison 2005, p. 102).

If none of the reasons that go to justify pardons based on mercy rather than on justice applies in the case of divine pardon, then it is difficult to see how God can mercifully pardon sins; indeed, it is difficult to see how divine pardon is possible at all, since neither can it be justified on grounds of justice. What seems to be needed is a way of reconciling divine mercy and justice that justifies a pardon without sacrificing the demands of either virtue.

3.3.3.4   Reconciliation of Divine Mercy and Justice

In fact, we seem to have backed into a persuasive argument for the conviction of Anselm and the Reformers that the satisfaction of divine justice is a necessary condition of salvation. Our inquiry suggests the following argument in support of the necessitarian perspective:

1. Necessarily (Retributive justice is essential to God).
2. Necessarily (If retributive justice is essential to God, then God justly punishes every sin).
3. Necessarily (If God justly punishes every sin, then divine justice is satisfied).
4. Therefore, necessarily (Divine justice is satisfied.)
5. Therefore, necessarily (If some human beings are saved, divine justice is satisfied).

Let me say a word about each of the premises.

In support of (1) we have seen that the centrality and prominence of divine retributive justice in the biblical scheme supports its being essential to God. Moreover, to mention an ad hominem consideration, neo–Socinian opponents of penal substitution need (1) if they are to argue successfully for the injustice of penal substitution, for otherwise God may determine that it is not unjust to punish a substitute in our place. Given that there is no higher law to which God must conform, He will be bound only by His own nature in determining what is just or unjust.

The support for (2) lies in the absence of any apparent justification for pardons of sheer mercy on God's part. It is difficult to see what would justify waiving the demands of retributive justice essential God's nature. We say "justly punishes" to ensure the truth of (3), since only proportionate punishment of sins committed will satisfy the demands of retributive justice.

From the three premises, (4) follows. Divine justice is satisfied so long as no sin goes unpunished. This will be the case whether there are no human beings and, hence, no sin, or whether there are in fact sinners. (5) in turn follows, since any proposition implies a necessary truth. It also follows that if divine justice is not satisfied, then no human beings are saved; indeed, that it is impossible that any human beings are saved.

If this is right, then God's pardoning us for our sins demands the satisfaction of God's justice. This is exactly what the atonement theories of Anselm and the Reformers offer. In the Reformers' view, Christ as our substitute and representative bears the punishment due for every sin, so that the demands of divine retributive justice are fully met. The demands of divine justice thus satisfied, God can in turn pardon us of our sins. God's pardon is thus predicated on Christ's satisfying for us the demands of divine retributive justice. Indeed, in a sense, such a divine pardon meets the requirements of even the pure retributivists, for given Christ's satisfaction of divine retributive justice on our behalf, nothing more is due from us. God's pardon of us is therefore required by justice. On the other hand, God's provision of Christ as our penal substitute is an active expression of God's mercy and grace, giving us what we did not deserve. The whole scheme is motivated by and justified by God's grace: "For by grace you have been saved through faith, and this is not your own doing; it is the gift of God – not the result of works, so that no one may boast" (Eph 2.8–9). This atoning arrangement is a gift of God to us, not based on human merit. In this sense God's pardon of us, while consistent with divine justice, is a pardon grounded ultimately in mercy.

3.3.4 Redemption and Sanctification

Redemption should be augmented by other motifs that we have not had space to address, such as new creation (II Cor 5.17). Atonement from sin is a forensic transaction, which would be powerless to transform our lives without the work of the Holy Spirit in regeneration and sanctification. Our legal pardon by God no more transforms our character and makes us virtuous people than does a human pardon a convicted criminal. Legally freed from condemnation and imputed Christ's righteousness, we still need to be transformed by the ongoing work of the Spirit in infusing righteousness into us to make us, over time, into the men and women that God wants us to be. Sanctification is not a forensic transaction but a moral transformation of character and is not therefore wrought by divine pardon alone.

3.4 Moral Influence

Finally, as Abelard emphasized, Christ's death is the source of a moral influence upon humanity that helps to draw people to faith in Christ and to persevere in faith through trials and even martyrdom.

3.4.1 Moral Influence in Isolation

Taken in isolation, the moral influence theory is hopeless as an atonement theory. Not only is it biblically inadequate, but it is powerless to explain, for example, how redemption is accomplished for all those believers who lived prior to the time of Christ, upon whom his death had therefore no influence whatsoever. Moreover, once penal substitution has been removed, the moral influence theory becomes bizarre. In his classic work *The Atonement*, philosopher-theologian R. W. Dale mused,

> If my brother made his way into a burning house to save my child from the flames, and were himself to perish in his heroic venture, his fate would be a wonderful proof of his affection for me and mine; but if there were no child in the house, and if I were told that he entered it and perished with no other object than to show his love for me, the explanation would be absolutely unintelligible. (1884, p. liv; cf. Denney 1907, p. 177)

Penal substitution thus lies at the heart of the moral influence of the death of Christ.

3.4.2 Penal Substitution and Moral Influence

Non-necessitarian penal substitution theorists like Hugo Grotius have especially stressed the moral influence of Christ's substitutionary death, which motivated God's contingent choice of satisfying His justice through penal substitution. Blaine Swen, for example, sees in penal substitution God's provision of both disincentives for human beings to continue in their sinful state of alienation from God and positive incentives for them to embrace God's offer of reconciliation (Swen 2012, pp. 165–75). Christ's making satisfaction through penal substitution discourages persistence in a state of alienation from God in two ways: (i) penal substitution, by showing God's wrath upon sin, alerts sinners to the danger of their remaining in a state of alienation from God; and (ii) God, by insisting on exacting so high a price of salvation at Christ's hand, demonstrates the high value of His offer of salvation. Christ's making satisfaction through penal substitution encourages sinners to embrace God's offer of forgiveness in three ways: (i) penal substitution demonstrates God's objectively expunging a person's guilt, thereby helping him to overcome his sense of shame; (ii) penal substitution demonstrates God's justice, thereby encouraging victims of injustice to be open to a loving relationship with God; (iii) penal substitution demonstrates God's love of sinners, as He substitutes Himself for them in bearing their just desert, thereby encouraging in turn a loving response to Him.

Although for Grotians such benefits play a more crucial role in motivating God's choice of penal substitution than they do in necessitarian theories, still it is evident that such disincentives to persistence in alienation from God and incentives to freely embracing God's offer of forgiveness will attend necessitarian theories as well. And, of course, even on necessitarian theories, God's choosing the particular means of Christ's substitutionary punishment remains contingent, in which case Christ's passion may be motivated by its production of such benefits.

The moral influence upon mankind of Christ's self-sacrificial death is truly inestimable. Repeatedly represented figuratively in literature and graphically in art, the death of Christ has, even more than his teaching, more than his character, made Jesus of Nazareth an arresting and captivating person for hundreds of millions, if not billions, of people and has inspired countless people to bear with courage and faith terrible pain and even death. As mentioned earlier, it is not at all implausible that only in a world that includes such an atoning death would the optimal number of people come freely to love and know God and so to find eternal life. God's wisdom, not only His love and holiness, is thus manifest in the atoning death of Christ.

References

Abelard, Peter. (2011). *Commentary on Paul's Epistle to the Romans.* The Fathers of the Church, Mediaeval Continuation 12, Steven Cartwright, ed., Washington, DC: Catholic University of America Press.

Anselm. (1962). "Cur Deus homo." In S. N. Deane, trans., *Saint Anselm: Basic Writings*, 2nd edn. La Salle, IL: Open Court, pp. 191–302.

Augustine. (1865). "*De Agone Christiano* [On the Christian Struggle]." In J. P. Migne, ed., *Patrologia Latina* 40. Paris: Garnier fratres, cols. 289–310. http://www.augustinus.it/latino/agone_cristiano/index.htm.

Augustine. (1887). *On the Trinity.* Nicene and Post-Nicene Fathers 1/3, Philip Schaff, ed., New York: The Christian Literature Company.

Aulén, Gustaf. (1969). *Christus Victor: An Historical Study of the Three Main Types of the Idea of the Atonement*, New York: Macmillan.

Bailey, Daniel P. (1998). "Concepts of *Stellvertretung* in the Interpretation of Isaiah 53." In William H. Bellinger, Jr. and William R. Farmer, eds., *Jesus and the Suffering Servant: Isaiah 53 and Christian Origins*. Harrisburg, PA: Trinity Press International, pp. 223–50.

Bailey, Daniel P. (forthcoming). "Atonement in the Hebrew Bible, early Judaism, and the New Testament: An overview." *Biblical Research*, 62.

Brien, Andrew. (1998). "Mercy within legal justice." *Social Theory and Practice*, 24(1), pp. 83–110.

Calvin, John. (1972). *Institutes of the Christian Religion*, 2 vols., Henry Beveridge, trans., Grand Rapids, MI: Wm. B. Eerdmans.

Caplow, Stacy. (2013). "Governors! Seize the law: A call to expand the use of pardons to provide relief from deportation." *Boston University Public Interest Law Journal* 22: 293–339.

Carson, D. A. (2004). "Atonement in Romans 3:21–26." In Charles E. Hill and Frank A. James III, eds., *The Glory of the Atonement: Biblical, Historical, and Practical Perspectives*. Downers Grove, IL: InterVarsity Press, pp. 119–39.

Craig, William Lane. (2001). *Time and Eternity: Exploring God's Relationship to Time*, Wheaton, IL: Crossway.

Crisp, Oliver D. (2009). "Original Sin and Atonement." In Thomas P. Flint and Michael C. Rea, eds., *The Oxford Handbook of Philosophical Theology.* Oxford: Oxford University Press, pp. 430–51.

Crisp, Oliver. (2011). "Salvation and Atonement: On the Value and Necessity of the Work of Jesus Christ." In Ivor J. Davidson and Murray A. Rae, eds.,

The God of Salvation: Soteriology in Theological Perspective. Farnham: Ashgate, pp. 105–20.

Crouch, Jeffrey. (2009). *The Presidential Pardon Power*, Lawrence, KS: University Press of Kansas.

Dale, R. W. (1884). *The Atonement*, 9th edn, London: Hodder & Stoughton.

Denney, James. (1907). *The Death of Christ: Its Place and Interpretation in the New Testament*, London: Hodder and Stoughton.

Dunn, James D. G. (2008). "The New Perspective: Whence, What and Whither?" In *The New Perspective on Paul*, rev. edn. Grand Rapids, MI: Wm. B. Eerdmans, pp. 1–97.

Eusebius of Caesarea. (1920). *Demonstration of the Gospel*. In Ferrar, W. J., trans. *The Proof of the Gospel, Being the Demonstratio Evangelica of Eusebius of Caesarea*. Vol. 2. New York: The Macmillan Company.

Farmer, William R. (1998). "Reflections on Isaiah 53 and Christian Origins." In William H. Bellinger, Jr. and William R. Farmer, eds., *Jesus and the Suffering Servant: Isaiah 53 and Christian Origins*. Harrisburg, PA: Trinity Press International, pp. 260–80.

Feinberg, Joel. (1970). "The Expressive Function of Punishment." In *Doing and Deserving: Essays in the Theory of Responsibility*. Princeton: Princeton University Press, pp. 95–118.

Feinberg, Joel and Gross, Hyman, eds. (1980). *Philosophy of Law*, 2nd edn., Belmont, CA: Wadsworth.

Finlan, Steven. (2007). *Options on Atonement in Christian Thought*, Collegeville, MN: Liturgical Press.

Fuller, Lon L. (1930). "Legal fictions." *Illinois Law Review*, 25(4), pp. 363–99.

Fuller, Lon L. (1931a). "Legal fictions." *Illinois Law Review*, 25(4), pp. 513–46.

Fuller, Lon L. (1931b). "Legal fictions." *Illinois Law Review*, 25(4), pp. 877–910.

Gathercole, Simon. (2015). *Defending Substitution: An Essay on Atonement in Paul*, Grand Rapids, MI: Baker Academic.

Gomes, Alan. (1990). "Faustus Socinus' '*De Jesu Christo Servatore*,' Part III: Historical introduction, translation and critical notes." Ph.D. dissertation. Ann Arbor, MI: University Microfilms International.

Green, Joel B. (2006). "Kaleidoscopic View." In James Beilby and Paul R. Eddy, eds., *The Nature of the Atonement*. Downers Grove, IL: IVP Academic, pp. 157–85.

Gregory of Nyssa. (1893). *The Great Catechism*. Nicene and Post-Nicene Fathers 2/5, Philip Schaff and Henry Wace, eds. New York: The Christian Literature Company.

Grotius, Hugo. (1889). *A Defence of the Catholic Faith concerning the Satisfaction of Christ, against Faustus Socinus*, Frank Hugh Foster, trans., Andover, MA: Warren F. Draper.

Heicke, Thomas. (2016). "Participation and Abstraction in the Yom Kippur Ritual according to Leviticus 16." Paper presented to the "Ritual in the Biblical World" section of the Society of Biblical Literature, San Antonio, TX, November 21.

Hermisson, Hans-Jürgen. (2004). "The Fourth Servant Song in the Context of Second Isaiah." In Bernd Janowski and Peter Stuhlmacher, eds., *The Suffering Servant: Isaiah 53 in Jewish and Christian Sources.* Grand Rapids: Eerdmans, pp. 16–47.

Hill, Daniel J. and Jedwab, Joseph. (2015). "Atonement and the Concept of Punishment." In Oliver D. Crisp and Fred Sanders, eds., *Locating Atonement: Explorations in Constructive Dogmatics.* Grand Rapids, MI: Zondervan, pp. 139–53.

Hofius, Otfried. (2004). "The Fourth Servant Song in the New Testament Letters." In Bernd Janowski and Peter Stuhlmacher, eds., *The Suffering Servant: Isaiah 53 in Jewish and Christian Sources.* Grand Rapids: Eerdmans, pp. 163–88.

Husak, Douglas. (2005). "*Malum Prohibitum* and Retributivism." In R. A. Duff and Stuart P. Green, eds., *Defining Crimes: Essays on the Special Part of the Criminal Law,* Oxford Monographs on Criminal Law and Justice, Oxford: Oxford University Press, pp. 65–90.

Irons, Charles Lee. (2015). *The Righteousness of God: A Lexical Examination of the Covenant-Faithfulness Interpretation,* Wissenschaftliche Untersuchungen zum Neuen Testament II 386, Tübingen: Mohr Siebeck.

Kobil, Daniel T. (1991). "The quality of mercy strained: wresting the pardoning power from the king." *Texas Law Review*, 69, pp. 569–641.

Leftow, Brian. (2012). *God and Necessity,* Oxford: Oxford University Press.

Leigh, L. H. (1982). *Strict and Vicarious Liability: A Study in Administrative Criminal Law,* Modern Legal Studies, London: Sweet and Maxwell.

Lewis, David. (1997). "Do we believe in penal substitution?" *Philosophical Papers*, 26(3), pp. 203–09.

Lind, Douglas. (2015). "The Pragmatic Value of Legal Fictions." In Maksymilian Del Mar and William Twining, eds., *Legal Fictions in Theory and Practice.* Law and Philosophy Library 110. Switzerland: Springer Verlag, pp. 83–109.

Luther, Martin. (1939). *Commentary on St. Paul's Epistle to the Galatians,* Theodore Graebner, trans., Christian Classics Ethereal Library. Grand Rapids, MI: Zondervan.

Marshall, I. Howard. (2007). *Aspects of the Atonement: Cross and Resurrection in the Reconciling of God and Humanity*, London: Paternoster.

Messing, Noah A. (2016). "A new power?: Civil offenses and presidential clemency." *Buffalo Law Review*, 64, pp. 661–743.

Milgrom, Jacob. (1991). *Leviticus 1–16*. The Anchor Bible 3. New York: Doubleday.

Mitros, Joseph F. (1967). "Patristic views of Christ's salvific work." *Thought*, 42(3), pp. 415–47.

Moore, Kathleen Dean. (1989). *Pardons: Justice, Mercy, and the Public Interest*, Oxford: Oxford University Press.

Moore, Michael. (1997). *Placing Blame: A Theory of Criminal Law*, Oxford: Oxford University Press.

Moreland, J. P. and Craig, William Lane. (2017). *Philosophical Foundations for a Christian Worldview*, 2nd edn., Downers Grove, IL: InterVarsity Press.

Morison, Samuel T. (2005). "The politics of grace: On the moral justification of executive clemency." *Buffalo Criminal Law Review*, 9(1), pp. 1–138.

Morris, Leon. (1983). *The Atonement: Its Meaning and Significance*, Downers Grove, IL: InterVarsity Press.

Murphy, Jeffrie G. (1985). "Retributivism, moral education, and the liberal state." *Criminal Justice Ethics*, 4, pp. 3–11.

Murphy, Mark C. (2009). "Not penal substitution but vicarious punishment." *Faith and Philosophy* 26(3), pp. 253–73.

Nazianzus, Gregory. (1894). *Select Orations*. Nicene and Post-Nicene Fathers 2/7, Philip Schaff and Henry Wace, eds., New York: The Christian Literature Company.

Origen. (1935). *Origenes Werke: Die Griechischen Christlichen Schriftsteller der ersten drei Jahrhunderte*. Ernst Benz and Erich Klostermann, eds., *Origenes Matthäuserklärung* 10. Leipzig: J. C. Heinrichs'sche Buchhandlung.

Ormerod, David. (2011). *Smith and Hogan's Criminal Law*, 13th edn., Oxford: Oxford University Press.

Owen, John. (n.d.). *A Dissertation on Divine Justice: or, the Claims of Vindicatory Justice Asserted*. London: L. J. Higham and J. Murgatroyd.

Plantinga, Alvin. (2011). "Comments on 'Satanic Verses: Moral Chaos in Holy Writ'." In Michael Bergmann, Michael J. Murray, and Michael C. Rea, eds., *Divine Evil?: The Moral Character of the God of Abraham*. Oxford: Oxford University Press, pp. 109–14.

Porter, Steven J. (2004). "Swinburnian atonement and the doctrine of penal substitution." *Faith and Philosophy*, 21(2), pp. 228–41.

Prior, A. N. (1958). "The syntax of time-distinctions." *Franciscan Studies*, 18(2), pp. 105–20.

Quinn, Philip L. (2004). "Review of *Papers in Ethics and Social Philosophy* by David Lewis." *Noûs*, 38(4), pp. 711–30.

Ripstein, Arthur. (2002). "Philosophy of Tort Law." In Jules Coleman and Scott Shapiro, eds., *The Oxford Handbook of Jurisprudence and Philosophy of Law*. Oxford: Oxford University Press, pp. 656–86.

Rivière, Jean. (1909). *The Doctrine of the Atonement: A Historical Essay*. Vol. 1. Luigi Cappadelta, trans., London: Kegan Paul, Trench, Trübner & Co.

Roberts, H. R. T. (1971). "Mercy." *Philosophy*, 46(178), pp. 352–53.

Ruane, Nicole. (2016). "Constructing Contagion on Yom Kippur: Reflections on the Scapegoat as Hatta't." Paper presented to the "Ritual in the Biblical World" section of the Society of Biblical Literature, San Antonio, TX, November 21.

Schauer, Frederick. (2015). "Legal Fictions Revisited." In Maksymilian Del Mar and William Twining, eds., *Legal Fictions in Theory and Practice*. Law and Philosophy Library 110. Switzerland: Springer Verlag, 113–30.

Schoenburg, Samuel E. (2016). "Clemency, war powers, and Guantánamo." *New York University Law Review*, 91, pp. 917–53.

Sklar, Jay. (2015). *Sin, Impurity, Sacrifice, Atonement: The Priestly Conceptions*, Sheffield, UK: Sheffield Phoenix Press.

Smart, Alwynne. (1968). "Mercy." *Philosophy*, 43(166), pp. 345–59.

Smeaton, George. (1957). *The Doctrine of the Atonement, as Taught by the Apostles*, Edinburgh: T. & T. Clark, 1870. Rep. edn., *The Apostles' Doctrine of the Atonement*, Grand Rapids, MI: Zondervan.

Steiner, Ashley M. (1997). "Remission of guilt or removal of punishment? The effects of a presidential pardon." *Emory Law Journal*, 46, pp. 959–1003

Stump, Eleonore. (2018). *Atonement*, Oxford: Oxford University Press.

Swen, Blaine. (2012). "The Logic of Divine-Human Reconciliation: A Critical Analysis of Penal Substitution as an Explanatory Feature of Atonement." Ph.D. dissertation. Loyola University, Chicago.

Tonry, Michael, ed. (2011). *Retributivism Has a Past; Has It a Future?* Studies in Penal Theory and Philosophy, Oxford: Oxford University Press.

Turretin, Francis. (1992). *Institutes of Elenctic Theology*, 3 vols., George Musgrave Giger, trans., James T. Dennison, ed., Phillipsburg, N.J: Presbyterian and Reformed.

Vaihinger, Hans. (1949). *The Philosophy of 'As if'*, C. K. Ogden, trans., 2nd edn., International Library of Psychology, Philosophy, and Scientific Method, London: Routledge & Kegan Paul.

Walen, Alec. (2014). "Retributive Justice." In Edward N. Zalta, ed., *Stanford Encyclopedia of Philosophy.* Summer 2014 edn. http://plato.stanford.edu /entries/justice-retributive/.

Watts, Rikki E. (1998). "Jesus's Death, Isaiah 53, and Mark 10:45: *A Crux Revisited.*" In William H. Bellinger, Jr. and William R. Farmer, eds., *Jesus and the Suffering Servant: Isaiah 53 and Christian Origins.* Harrisburg, PA: Trinity Press International, pp. 125–51.

Weihofen, Henry. (1939). "The effect of a pardon." *University of Pennsylvania Law Review,* 88, pp. 177–93.

White, Mark D., ed. (2011). *Retributivism: Essays on Theory and Policy,* Oxford: Oxford University Press.

Williston, Samuel. (1915). "Does a pardon blot out guilt?" *Harvard Law Review,* 28(7), pp. 647–63.

Zaibert, Leo. (2006). *Punishment and Retribution.* Aldershot, Hants: Ashgate.

Cambridge Elements ☰

The Philosophy of Religion

Yujin Nagasawa
University of Birmingham

Yujin Nagasawa is Professor of Philosophy and Co-Director of the John Hick Centre for Philosophy of Religion at the University of Birmingham. He is the author of *God and Phenomenal Consciousness: A Novel Approach to Knowledge Arguments* (Cambridge University Press, 2008).

About the series

This Cambridge Elements series provides concise and structured introductions to all the central topics in the philosophy of religion. The books in the series are written by distinguished senior scholars and bright junior scholars with relevant expertise. This series offers balanced, comprehensive coverage of multiple perspectives in the philosophy of religion.

Cambridge Elements ≡

The Philosophy of Religion

A full series listing is available at: www.cambridge.org/core/series/elements-in-the-philosophy-of-religion

Printed in the United States
By Bookmasters